Proof From The Top

Why This Book Matters

"Winning Business Secrets is more than a leadership book, it's a mirror, a blueprint, and a masterclass in courageous transformation. Sherry Winn writes with the kind of clarity and heart that only comes from lived experience. Her stories cut through the noise, and her insights are battle-tested from Olympic courts to boardrooms. If you're ready to lead with grit, vision, and unapologetic authenticity, this book will guide you every step of the way."

Tara LaFon Gooch,
International TEDx Speaker, 2X Bestselling Author,
CEO of Best Branding Solutions

"Sherry scores for leaders at every stage of their journey. Her book offers deep insights and actionable strategies for leading with purpose—whether starting out, shaping a team, or creating a legacy. A must-read for those committed to driving meaningful change."

Richard Lowney,
Founder/CEO,
Clearview Software International, Inc.

Sherry's new book, Winning Business Secrets, is a total game-changer! True to who she is, Sherry leans all the way into vulnerability, sharing real-life experiences that hit home. This isn't fluff—it's packed with life-changing truths, clear steps to success, and powerful takeaways. If you're ready for a real blueprint (from someone who walks the walk), dig in. You'll be better for it!

Tracie Kenyon,
former CEO,
Montana Credit Union League

If you're looking for actionable leadership advice that is fresh and heart-centered, Sherry Winn's "Winning Business Secrets" needs to be on your shelf. Sherry Winn provides you with the blueprint to unlock genius in your team—and, more importantly, in yourself (because to have a great team, you must have a great leader).

Nadya Rousseau,
Founder/CEO,
Alter New Media

"If you want the secrets to building a winning leadership style, Sherry Winn has the nuts-and-bolts answers. Presented through raw personal stories and client interactions, Sherry provides practical information in a way that is realistic to the challenges leaders face daily. Winning Business Secrets is the handbook every executive leader should be given on their first day but isn't. As someone who researches and trains leadership for a living, I would recommend this book anytime!"

Dr. Melissa Robinson-Winemiller,
Leadership Consultant & Doctoral Researcher

Winning Business Secrets is packed with real-life stories and practical insights that make the lessons both relatable and usable. Sherry Winn doesn't just share leadership theory—she brings it to life through pointed examples and an actionable narrative that leaders at any level can apply right away. A clear, honest guide for building stronger teams and closing bigger deals with greater confidence.

Dr. Robyn Lynette,
MentalMacGyver.com,
Hardwired to Grow

Winning Business Secrets

How to Build Leaders Who Succeed, Gain Bigger Deals
Faster, and Double The Genius Factor of Your Teams

Sherry Winn

Contents

10% of all royalties are donated to:
The Yellowstone Wildlife Sanctuary whose mission is the protection and conservation of the Yellowstone ecosystem wildlife and natural habitats. To discover more, visit:

www.yellowstonewildlifesanctuary.com

Foreword

When Sherry first approached me about her work on leadership development, my first reaction was "we'll see". As someone who has spent decades in the business, government, and civic trenches, I've seen countless leadership trends come and go—many built on theory or even conjecture rather than tested practice. Many are created as a hook to sell a book. As I delved into the manuscript that would become this book, and as I came to know and understand who Sherry Winn is at her core, I discovered I did not need to wait long. I could quickly "see" the value. The leadership insights forged in the crucible of real experience are triumphant and lift the eyes of any reader to a higher calling.

What sets "Winning Business Secrets" apart is its refreshing honesty. Sherry doesn't pretend leadership is easy or that there's a simple five-step formula for success. Instead, she invites us into the messy, complicated, and ultimately rewarding journey of authentic leadership. From her experiences as a championship basketball coach and Olympic athlete to her work with executives across industries and organizations, she demonstrates that true leadership isn't about having all the answers—it's about asking better questions and creating environments where everyone can thrive. It is about self-leadership first. It is about a life's global journey, not just a weekend pleasure trip. It is about rising above being "scared, hurt, and deeply affected" by challenges, personal insults, and even failures to emerge as a trusted, confident, human being – who leads with purpose.

The principles in these pages have already transformed organizations I've witnessed firsthand. I've seen struggling teams become cohesive powerhouses using her approaches to diversity and hybrid workforce management. I've observed leaders who were once rigid and controlling evolve into adaptive forces that inspire innovation and collaboration. Most importantly, I've watched as accountability shifted from a dreaded word to a celebrated practice within companies that embraced her methods.

What I appreciate most about Sherry is that she sets aside rote and damaging monikers and mandates that proliferate division and often hatred in our society – it's not "about numbers or checking boxes". She approaches the need for diversity away from political dogma but rather as the opportunity to learn from people with differing environments, experience, educations, and enlightenments to make organizations triumphant with rich culture and creativity. Setting aside mandates, embracing the brilliance of others who are "not like us" makes us more brilliant. Following Sherry's insights creates a better world, not just better organizations.

What I appreciate most about Sherry's approach is that it's both practical and profound. This isn't just another theoretical leadership tome; it's a blueprint for action. Each chapter contains not only compelling stories and insights but also concrete steps for implementation—her "Winning Takeaways" and "Winning Success Steps" ensure that this book isn't just read but lived.

For years, in organizations where I have influence, we have enacted the practice of holding weekly stand-up fifteen-minute meetings to do book reviews. We purchase a book for everyone in the organization (text or audio). We then read them together and assign a chapter a week to someone in the organization to present the insights of the book to everyone in the company for small organizations or to their division/department for larger organizations. We have two rules: 1) the presentation must focus on what was learned that will make the organization better (blunt but benevolent candor is encouraged), and 2) everyone in the group must get slides from the presentation to create a library of learning for organizational improvement. This book will now become one of the mandatory "book club" books to be reviewed annually.

Whether you're leading a multinational corporation, a growing startup, or simply yourself, the wisdom in these pages will challenge you to look beyond conventional leadership practices and embrace a more human, more effective approach to guiding others. In a business world that often prioritizes metrics over meaning, Sherry reminds us that the greatest leaders succeed not just because of what they know, but because of how they connect.

I'm honored to introduce this remarkable work. It will guide all of us to "finish stronger than we start". It will help "turn vision into victory". I'm confident that the journey you're about to embark on will transform your leadership practice, your understanding of what's possible when you lead with both strategy and heart, and who you are at your core in this vast experience called life.

Paul Clayson
Executive Chairman
Valuation Impact

The High-Performance Leadership Blueprint

Welcome to the Dance

Let's be honest—leadership books are a dime a dozen. They crowd bookstore shelves with promises of five easy steps to become the next Steve Jobs or Brené Brown, as if transformational leadership were as simple as following a recipe for chocolate chip cookies. (Spoiler alert: it's not.)

So why am I adding another leadership book to the pile? Because after decades as a championship basketball coach, Olympic athlete, and leadership coach to some of the most influential executives across the globe, I've learned something profound: **real leadership isn't about having all the answers—it's about asking better questions**.

This isn't your typical leadership manual filled with theoretical frameworks that look impressive but fall apart in the real world. This is a blueprint built in the trenches, tested under pressure, and proven in the arena where results—not intentions—are the only measure of success.

My Leadership Journey (The Unfiltered Version)

I'd love to tell you I've always been an enlightened leader with impeccable emotional intelligence, but that would be a lie big enough to make Pinocchio blush. The truth? I was a control freak who thought leadership meant having an iron grip on every detail.

As a young basketball coach, I once had a complete meltdown before a national championship game because our pre-game meal was served late, throwing off my meticulously planned schedule by thirty minutes. I was breathing fire, my anxiety infecting the entire team like a bad case of the flu. Somehow, we still won that championship—despite my leadership, not because of it.

It took me years (and more than a few spectacular failures) to realize that true leadership isn't about control—it's about connection. It's not about being perfect; it's about being present. And it's definitely not about having all the power; it's about empowering others.

My journey from taskmaster to transformational leader wasn't a straight line. It was more like trying to parallel park a bus on a San Francisco hill during an earthquake—messy, uncomfortable, and with plenty of moments where I wanted to abandon the vehicle altogether.

What You'll Discover in These Pages

This book is organized into the critical dimensions of high-performance leadership, each chapter revealing essential truths that have transformed organizations and leaders worldwide:

The Leadership North Star: How to define your guiding purpose and align your team around a compelling vision that inspires commitment, not just compliance.

Diversity: The Alchemy of a High-Performance Team: Why the most innovative and resilient teams embrace differences in thought, background, and perspective—and how to build truly inclusive cultures.

Embracing the Hybrid Workforce: Practical strategies for leading teams across physical and virtual spaces, creating connection without proximity.

The Art of Hiring High Performers: How to identify and attract people who don't just fill positions but elevate your entire organization.

Cultivating the Genius Factor of Your Team: Techniques to unlock the untapped potential within your team members, pushing them beyond their perceived limitations.

The Heartbeat of Leadership: Why emotional connections are the foundation of influence, and how to lead with both strength and heart.

Embracing Uncertainty: How to turn unpredictability into an advantage by making adaptability your superpower.

Driving Change Through Accountability: The transformative power of ownership at every level of your organization.

As we explore these dimensions together, I'll share stories of both triumph and disaster—from Olympic competitions to corporate boardrooms, from championship games to challenging coaching sessions. These aren't sanitized case studies; they're raw, real experiences with lessons that stuck because they occasionally hurt.

Why This Book Is Different

Look, I'm not going to pretend this book contains some magical leadership secret that will transform you overnight into a cross between Gandhi and Jeff Bezos. What it does offer is honesty, practical wisdom, and a roadmap for becoming the kind of leader people genuinely want to follow.

In my world, leadership isn't about looking good in the leadership suit—it's about results. It's about creating environments where people thrive, innovation flourishes, and performance soars. It's about making difficult decisions with both courage and compassion. And sometimes, it's about admitting you were wrong, adjusting course, and moving forward with greater wisdom.

Throughout these chapters, you'll meet remarkable leaders who embody these principles—people like Karen Halliday, who stood up for her team when an entire system was against them; Jason Holland, who transformed his personal struggle with addiction into a leadership philosophy built on humility and authenticity; and John Gardiner, who saved a sinking company by being "the realist at the optimism party."

How to Use This Book

You could read this book cover to cover like a novel, but I suggest a different approach. Start with the chapter that speaks to your most pressing leadership challenge. Each chapter concludes with "Winning Takeaways"—the essential principles distilled for immediate application—and "Winning Success Steps"—practical questions that turn insight into action.

Use these tools. Write in the margins. Challenge my assumptions. Apply these ideas in your world, not as rigid formulas but as frameworks that adapt to your unique circumstances.

The most valuable leadership lessons I've learned didn't come from books; they came from failing, reflecting, and trying again with new insight. My hope is that these pages will save you some of the painful lessons I had to learn the hard way.

A Final Word Before We Begin

Whether you're leading a multinational corporation, a small business, a nonprofit, or simply yourself, remember this: Leadership isn't a position—it's a practice. It's not about being in charge—it's about taking care of those in your charge.

The journey ahead will challenge you to look in the mirror before looking at your team, to embrace uncertainty rather than fear it, and to lead with both your head and your heart. It won't always be comfortable, but transformation rarely happens in the comfort zone.

So, let's begin this journey together—not as expert and novice, but as fellow travelers on the path of leadership. I promise to give you my unfiltered truth, practical tools, and occasionally, a much-needed reality check (delivered with love, of course).

Are you ready to become the leader your team deserves? Turn the page, and let's get started.

Chapter 1

The Leadership North Star: A Journey of Self and Team Discovery

The Leadership North Star

Leadership isn't about you, yet it starts with you. This paradox is the foundation of the Leadership North Star—your guiding light on the journey to self and team discovery. Imagine a captain setting sail without a compass. Even with the finest ship and crew, the journey would be aimless, marked by frustration and lost potential. As a leader, you are the captain, and your personal growth and self-awareness are your compass. To effectively lead others, you must first lead yourself. Without that foundation, how can you inspire trust, foster collaboration, or guide your team through challenges?

Learning The Lesson Through a New Lens

In 2012, I resigned as a college basketball coach without a future job opportunity. I was like Cortez burning the ships behind him so that his men could not retreat. There was no Plan B for me—make it or die. I had an idea that centered around becoming a speaker—one that I had little knowledge about other than knowing I was good at motivating my team. It was a good thing that I didn't know what I didn't know because 9 out of 10 speakers quit in their first year.

My North Star was an idea that wasn't fully conceptualized. I hadn't done my homework to understand that speaking wasn't about speaking as much as it was about marketing and running a business. I had zero skills in both of those.

But I had the one thing most people don't have—grit, the unwavering determination to make it happen.

My first paid speaking gig was in front of 2,000 people, and I was thrilled to be on stage as a paid speaker. Within the first five minutes, I realized I had lost the audience, and I still had 55 minutes left to stand in front of them, knowing that scrolling on their phones was more riveting than my words.

Then and there, I promised myself that losing an audience would never happen again. I hired a speaking coach and then another one. I got better. Then I hired a marketing coach and a business coach. Certainly, I improved through each one of these coaches, and yet my North Star remained a bit fuzzy.

For 23 years as a collegiate basketball coach, I helped my team develop a dream and practice toward living that dream. I coached them at visualizing success and pushing beyond the obstacles in front of them. Yet, I didn't know how to create my own Business North Star—the one that was clear, driven by goals, and a vision that inspired me beyond challenges.

The challenge for me was that I needed a business coach who would put me through steps one by one—a coach who understood how to teach. I needed processes broken down, not just conceptualized. A great coach knows how to break down skills, build them up in short steps so that success is experienced, and then put them all together in a game-like environment, which is what I did on the basketball court for 23 years.

I stumbled and bumbled along, gaining knowledge, getting better in my business and marketing efforts. I had become a phenomenal speaker, speaking for audiences as large as 14,000, yet I couldn't turn the corner on my business.

Then, I found a coach who challenged me by sending me 100 questions about my business. That's when I discovered I wasn't truly running a business—I had an incomplete North Star. I was excellent at speaking but had neglected the infrastructure, the systems, and the strategy that made a business sustainable.

That was the turning point. I dedicated myself to the same disciplined approach I had once used in coaching athletes. I treated my business like an elite team—setting clear objectives, tracking progress, and relentlessly fine-tuning my execution. I built processes that ensured consistency and growth. I refined my message to be both powerful and marketable. I established scalable systems that allowed me to increase my impact without burning out.

With each step, my North Star became clearer. It wasn't just about being a great speaker—it was about transforming leaders, organizations, and cultures. It was about creating lasting impact, not just delivering a powerful speech. And as I aligned with that vision, my business flourished.

Looking back, I realize that leadership—whether on the court, on the stage, or in the boardroom—is about having the courage to navigate uncertainty. It's about continuously refining your North Star, surrounding yourself with people who challenge you, and committing to the discipline of growth.

I had to learn what I had taught for years: No great team, no great leader, no great business succeeds without clarity, direction, and the perseverance to build something lasting. Today, my North Star is no longer incomplete. It shines brightly, guiding not just me, but the thousands of leaders I now help discover their own.

But clarity and direction don't come without struggling. Every leader's North Star is shaped by the trials they endure, the lessons they embrace, and the willingness to evolve.

Lessons from Matt Higgins: Vulnerability and Self-Awareness

During our interview, Matt Higgins, a trailblazer in his professional field and CEO of RSE Ventures, shared a compelling narrative of his rise and subsequent reckoning. "I experienced a meteoric rise in my career, much like the fictional character Doogie Howser—a teenage prodigy who became a licensed physician while navigating typical adolescent challenges," Matt explains. As the youngest press secretary in history, his trajectory appeared destined for uninterrupted success. Yet, life's unanticipated turbulence brought him to a stark realization. His publicized divorce and resulting psychotic break revealed not only a personal crisis but also a deeper understanding of his past lack of empathy. This profound shift became the foundation for his journey into self-awareness.

The Transformative Power of Introspection

Matt's story underscores an essential truth for leaders: growth stems from introspection and vulnerability. Reflecting on his experiences, Matt shares, "This personal crisis revealed my previous lack of empathy toward individuals facing trauma and adversity." His turning point is not merely a tale of recovery but a vital lesson in leadership. Through self-awareness, he began to unlock the answers he sought within himself, demonstrating the powerful role of inner reflection in achieving personal and professional transformation.

A significant insight from Matt's journey aligns with Abraham Maslow's theory of self-actualization. He notes, "Leaders who reach the pinnacle of their potential align with Maslow's concept of self-actualization—the fulfillment of one's capabilities and the desire for self-fulfillment." Such leaders, as Matt explains, are marked by grace and the courage to embrace their vulnerabilities. By openly sharing uncomfortable experiences, they create authentic connections with their teams, fostering trust and mutual respect. This alignment between self-awareness and leadership not only elevates individuals but also drives organizational excellence.

A Beacon for Leadership Growth

However, Matt's observations also highlight the consequences of a lack of self-awareness. He cautions, "Often, when teams struggle to progress, it's due to leaders adopting a dictatorial and autocratic style." These leaders, unaware of their impact, may inadvertently cultivate chaotic cultures, perpetuating cycles of dysfunction. The absence of introspection can lead to environments that require constant micromanagement, ultimately hindering both individual and organizational growth. Matt's reflections emphasize that self-awareness is not just a personal endeavor but a critical leadership competency.

Through his journey, Matt Higgins illustrates the transformative power of vulnerability and introspection in leadership. "Embracing vulnerability and introspection not only fosters personal growth but also cultivates healthier, more effective organizational cultures," he concludes. His story serves as a guiding beacon for leaders navigating their own challenges, urging them to seek the answers within. By doing so, they can chart a course toward self-actualization, creating a harmonious and resilient organizational culture where teams and individuals alike can thrive.

Gaining Clarity to Move the Needle Forward

One of my coaching clients, "Jamie," became exasperated with me one day during our call.

"You told me that you would help me find my way," Jamie said.

I replied, "I did say that. And you have to help me determine which way you want to go. What do you want to accomplish in the next year?"

Jamie shrugged. "I have no idea."

I tried again. "What's your biggest passion?"

"I don't know."

"Well," I said, "if you did know, what would it be?"

"I don't know."

"Okay," I said, leaning in, "if you could do anything in the world without worrying about time, money, or experience, what would you do?"

Jamie shook his head. "That isn't realistic, so it doesn't matter."

"Jamie, I can't help you if you don't help yourself. So, let's pretend I have a magic wand that erases all the reasons holding you back. What would you do if you could do anything?"

"Anything?"

"Yes, anything."

Jamie looked at me skeptically but finally answered, "I'd own a yacht and sail around the world. But I don't own a yacht, I don't have money for a yacht, and honestly, even if I did, I probably wouldn't buy it."

"Okay, then. What would you buy if you had enough money for a yacht?"

Jamie paused and then said, "If I had that kind of money, I'd help the local Boys and Girls Club. There are so many kids there who need help. If they got the right support, they could make a positive difference in the world. What I really want to do is make a positive impact."

"Let's start there, then."

Jamie blinked. "Where? How do we start changing the world? How do I help kids who are lost and without hope?"

I smiled. "We start with you."

"Me?"

"Yes, you. You can't give what you don't have. So, let's build you up first so that you can give more, and then more, and then even more."

Jamie hesitated. "But—"

I cut him off. "No more buts. If you have the passion to help others and make a difference, then let's begin with a different question: What can you do today to move six inches closer to your goal?"

"Six inches?" Jamie frowned. "But that's not very far."

"There you go again with the buts. No more buts! You're stopping yourself before you've even started. Let's focus on moving just six inches."

Jamie took a deep breath, exhaled slowly, and said, "Hmm. Six inches. All I have to do is move six inches from where I am today?"

"Yes."

"Okay. I need to get out of debt first."

"Let's not focus on getting out of debt. Let's focus on gaining money."

Jamie tilted his head. "What's the difference? Isn't that the same thing?"

"No. When you focus on getting out of debt, all your energy revolves around debt. Instead, focus on what you want, not what you don't want. So, how can you gain more money?"

Jamie thought for a moment. "I guess if I became a better salesperson, I could make higher commissions. Then I could allocate some money toward investments, some toward debt, and the rest for daily expenses."

"Perfect. Let's work on making you a better salesperson."

Jamie invested time in personal development and eventually became one of the top salespeople at his insurance company. Instead of spending his early earnings on himself, he invested over 30% of his income while diligently paying off his debt. During this time, he also volunteered as a mentor at local youth programs.

Jamie never bought a yacht, but he did take ten young kids on a dream ride, showing them that dreams are real—and possible all because he invested in himself first.

Life Lessons that Apply to Business

Our responsibility as leaders is to foster personal growth and to cultivate resilient organizations. During my conversation with Steve Hankins, CFO of Morgan Foods, Inc., he credited his grandfather with imparting invaluable life lessons that shaped his approach to success in business and life. His grandfather's teachings provided Steve with the essential toolset to learn how to guide from the North Star position. Here are the lessons he shared:

1. Always start with this question: How can I help you?

Steve's grandfather's unwavering commitment to service became the cornerstone of his success. When he approached clients, colleagues, or even family members, he always started with this question.

By approaching others with the question, "How can I help you?" we prioritize the needs of others and build trust. This question is not merely about politeness; it is a genuine offer to create value and foster collaboration. As leaders, when we put others first, we pave the way for deeper connections and mutual success.

2. Take the time to think deeply: Think. Think. Think.

"Don't rush into decisions," Steve's grandfather would often remind him. When faced with challenges, he encouraged Steve to pause and analyze the situation from every angle: think, think, think!

In our fast-paced world, where instant solutions are often rewarded, his advice for Steve to slow down and reflect was a game-changer. In leadership, decisions often carry significant consequences. Taking a moment to pause and analyze situations from every angle allows us to act with wisdom rather than haste. By embracing this practice, we unlock the potential for innovative solutions and avoid unnecessary mistakes.

3. Ensure everything is in order: Check. Check. Check.

Attention to detail was non-negotiable in Steve's grandfather's crop-dusting business, where even a minor oversight could lead to catastrophic consequences. He instilled in Steve the habit of double- and triple-checking his work, whether it was a financial report or a strategic plan.

Attention to detail is the hallmark of excellence. Whether it's a financial report or a strategic plan, double- and triple-checking ensures consistency and reliability. Excellence is not a single act but a habit of meticulous preparation. By adopting this principle, we set a standard of precision and accountability for ourselves and our teams.

4. Take care of your tools and resources: Take care of the equipment.

For Steve's grandfather, his crop-dusting planes were more than just machines; they were lifelines. He believed that taking care of your tools and resources was not optional but essential. This lesson extends beyond physical tools; it applies to time, energy, and even relationships.

Proper maintenance of resources—whether physical tools, time, energy, or relationships—ensures sustainability and peak performance. By valuing and preserving our assets, we demonstrate foresight and responsibility. As leaders, when we invest in the maintenance of our resources, we create a foundation for long-term success and resilience.

5. Be proactive: Look around to see what needs to be done, because something always needs to be done.

Steve's grandfather had a knack for staying one step ahead. He believed in the power of proactive leadership—the ability to anticipate needs and act before problems arise. On the farm, this meant fixing a fence before it broke or refueling a plane before it was empty.

Proactive leadership is about anticipating needs and addressing them before they become problems. Whether it's fixing a process or identifying opportunities for improvement, staying one step ahead fosters a culture of innovation and accountability. As leaders, when we take the initiative, we inspire our teams to do the same.

6. Stay engaged: Go on site. Offer suggestions on what can be improved.

Steve's grandfather taught him the value of staying engaged by being present and hands-on. Whether it was walking through the fields or visiting the hangar, he'd always take the time to observe and offer constructive feedback.

Leadership is not a spectator sport. Being present and engaged allows us to understand challenges firsthand and provide actionable feedback. Walking the floor, observing operations, and connecting with team members demonstrate commitment and build trust. By staying involved, we lead by example and create a culture of continuous improvement.

7. Commit to lifelong learning: Study your lessons. Learn everything about what you are doing.

Steve's grandfather's hunger for knowledge was insatiable. Despite not having formal education beyond high school, he immersed himself in learning everything about crop-dusting— from aviation mechanics to weather patterns. His example taught Steve that expertise is earned through dedication and curiosity.

Expertise is not innate; it is earned through dedication and curiosity. Continuous learning—whether through formal education, professional development, or self-directed study, we remain adaptable and informed. As leaders, when we embrace learning, we model the growth mindset needed to thrive in an ever-changing world.

8. Cultivate curiosity: Always be curious.

Curiosity was Steve's grandfather's secret weapon. He approached every situation with an open mind and a desire to learn. Curiosity is the spark that drives innovation. Asking questions like "Why does this work?" or "How can we make it better?" opens doors to new possibilities. When we approach situations with an open mind and a desire to learn, we fuel creativity and drive meaningful progress.

9. Lead with purpose: Be of service to other people.

For Steve's grandfather, leadership was never about power or prestige; it was about making a positive impact. True leadership is rooted in purpose. By serving others—whether mentoring a colleague or delivering results for stakeholders—we create a legacy of trust and shared success. Leadership with purpose builds a foundation of respect and drives meaningful change.

The wisdom Steve's grandfather shared serves as a powerful reminder that the principles of leadership are timeless. By embracing curiosity, fostering relationships, and committing to excellence, we can navigate the complexities of leadership with confidence and purpose. These lessons are not just Steve's to keep; they are an invitation for all of us to lead with intention and heart.

Steve may have earned his official MBA from college at the age of 22, but his unofficial degree—the one that truly set him up for success—came from his grandfather's wisdom. His guidance taught Steve that success is about embracing curiosity, fostering relationships, and staying committed to excellence. These principles are timeless and have become the foundation of Steve's personal and professional life.

The Leader's North Star: A Guide for Success

Understanding our North Star is critical because, as leaders, we are the direction for our teams. If we cannot guide ourselves toward success, our teams will fail. Knowing your purpose and passion are the two most critical steps to living your North Star. Carlos Vasquez's journey vividly illustrates this truth.

Overcoming Adversity: A Childhood of Hardship

Growing up in El Salvador, Carlos told me about the immense challenges he faced. He lived in a small hut without running water or electricity, eating simple meals of tortillas and, on lucky days, eggs from their chickens. Lawlessness and violence surrounded him, with frequent gunfights and piles of dead bodies serving as stark reminders of the instability. Seven powerful families controlled 90% of the country's wealth, a reality that forced his family to fight for survival.

The Relentless Pursuit of a Better Life

Despite these conditions, Carlos' mother worked tirelessly to bring him to the United States. When he arrived, he didn't speak a word of English but threw himself into hard work to support his family. By his early twenties, he was earning over $100,000 a year selling long-term care insurance for John Hancock. Yet, life continued to challenge him. A soccer injury led to blood clots that cost him his job, and severe COVID-19 nearly cost him his life. Through sheer determination, he recovered remarkably quickly, even returning to the soccer field within a week. Then, his wife left him—a turning point that forced Carlos to reevaluate his life's direction.

Finding Purpose Through Pain

Reflecting on his journey, Carlos found clarity in his North Star. "Through the pain and loss, I discovered a greater purpose: to change lives. My focus shifted from making money to becoming a better person and helping others. I realized that every hardship had shaped me, giving me the strength and perspective to inspire others." His story exemplifies how aligning with our North Star requires self-discovery, resilience, and a commitment to something greater than ourselves. It is through this alignment that we can lead with authenticity and empower our teams to thrive.

Winning Takeaways

- **Self-Leadership Precedes Team Leadership:** To guide others effectively, you must first develop your own self-awareness and clarity of purpose.
- **Embrace the Journey of Growth:** Finding your North Star is an iterative process that requires continuous learning, adaptation, and the courage to face your shortcomings.
- **Vulnerability Builds Authentic Leadership:** Embracing your vulnerabilities and sharing them appropriately creates deeper connections with your team and fosters a culture of trust.
- **Progress Comes in Small Steps:** Focus on moving "six inches" at a time toward your goals rather than being overwhelmed by the distance to your destination.
- **Shift from Problems to Solutions:** Direct your energy toward what you want to achieve rather than what you want to avoid—focus on gaining rather than losing.
- **Service-Oriented Leadership Builds Trust:** Begin every interaction with "How can I help you?" to create meaningful relationships and mutual success.
- **Personal Hardship Refines Leadership Purpose:** The challenges you overcome often reveal your deepest values and most authentic direction.

Winning Success Steps

- **Define Your Current Reality:** Where are you now in your leadership journey? What are your strengths and areas for growth? How clear is your personal North Star?

- Identify Your Purpose Beyond Profit: What impact do you want to make that transcends financial success? How does this purpose align with your deepest values?
- Plan Your Six-Inch Victory: What is one small action you can take today that moves you toward your leadership goals? How can you make this action specific and measurable?
- Reflect on Your Leadership Legacy: What wisdom or principles do you want to pass on to others? How are you currently embodying these principles in your leadership practice?
- Assess Your Self-Awareness: How well do you understand your impact on others? What feedback mechanisms can you implement to increase your self-awareness as a leader?

BONUS LEADERSHIP RESOURCES True influence starts with emotional connection. Use these three heart-centered leadership assessments to deepen trust, strengthen loyalty, and lead with both power and vulnerability.

Scan the QR code for your leadership-from-the-heart assessments.

Email me at
sherry@thewinningleadershipcompany.com
to book a **free** 45-minute session.

People don't follow titles. They follow truth.

Chapter 2

Diversity

The Alchemy of a High-Performance Team

From Division to Unity: Lessons in Empathy and Teamwork

The year was 1982, and I was sitting at a long table in Budapest, Hungary, surrounded by my USA National Team Handball teammates. We were eating dinner, gearing up for our games at the World Championships. The conversation shifted to sexual orientation, and our goalie made a comment I will never forget: "All gay people should be placed on an island, and it should be blown up."

Her words hit me like a punch to the gut. She didn't know it, but she was talking about me. In that moment, I felt condemned, unworthy of existing. The wounds her comment left were deep and personal. Yet, I said nothing—not that day or any day after. She seemed completely oblivious to the division her words had created, moving on as though nothing had happened.

But I couldn't move on. I avoided her as much as possible, keeping our interactions strictly professional. I wasn't rude, but I certainly wasn't friendly. On the court, I did my job—I would never let an opponent get past me and leave her vulnerable in goal—but that extra effort, the drive to push harder for my teammate, just wasn't there.

For years, I kept my distance. I didn't try to undermine her, but I wasn't in her corner, either. She wasn't getting my vote on anything. Then, six years later, I overheard her on a phone call speaking against my potential appointment as assistant national team coach. When she realized I was in the next room and had heard her, she tried to explain. But I wasn't ready to hear her out. Her words from all those years ago were still fresh in my mind. She had condemned the very essence of who I was, and reconciliation in that moment wasn't possible.

Looking back, maybe I could've handled things differently. Maybe I could have found a way to forgive. But at the time, I was still scared, hurt, and deeply affected by her words. That pain stuck with me, and it created a barrier—not just between us but within our team.

This experience taught me an important lesson: when we are separated, ostracized, or condemned for who we are, it becomes nearly impossible to form the kind of bonds that make a team successful. Whether it's our differences in culture, sexual identity, religion, or politics, when we're on the same team, we must find a way to work together. Without unity, everyone suffers while motivation dwindles, productivity declines, and the culture becomes one of isolation instead of connection. Diversity is more than tolerating differences; diversity is about finding strength in them and building something greater together.

Shifting The Comfort of Familiarity to Grow Team Dynamics

This understanding of unity and diversity extends beyond personal relationships and into organizational dynamics. Just as individuals thrive when differences are acknowledged and respected, teams and companies reach their highest potential when they embrace diversity in all its forms. However, achieving this requires intentional effort, as human nature often leans toward the comfort of familiarity. This tendency can create blind spots, especially in hiring practices, where the allure of "fitting in" may overshadow the value of bringing fresh perspectives and new ideas to the table.

Human nature tends to gravitate towards familiarity and routine. Just as we might find comfort in ordering the same latte from our local coffee shop, organizations often default to a "stick to what you know" mindset when hiring. If Employee X fits seamlessly into the team, the inclination is to replicate that success by hiring more of the same. However, this approach can inadvertently stifle diversity of thought and hinder a company's full potential.

The consequence? A workforce that mirrors itself—homogeneous in thought, action, and perspective. While this may foster cohesion, it also erects barriers to innovation and growth. Bold ideas emerge from the clash of diverse viewpoints, not from the echo chamber of conformity. Consider revolutionary inventions like the iPod or the smartphone—they have sprung from teams unafraid to challenge conventions, to explore the uncharted, and to embrace failure as a precursor to success.

The Broad Spectrum of Diversity

Diversity encompasses more than just race or gender; it encompasses a spectrum of identities and experiences. Research shows that diverse teams outperform homogeneous ones, driving innovation and financial success. Yet, achieving diversity requires intentional effort and systemic change.

While speaking with Jenna Pipchuk, CRO of the CRO Syndicate, she captured the essence of why diversity matters. "Diversity is essential for fostering innovation and creating an environment of psychological safety. The dynamics of how individuals collaborate are crucial, as each person's unique identity significantly influences team success." It's not just about checking boxes or meeting quotas; it's about creating a culture where innovation thrives and teams feel safe to share, challenge, and grow together. Diversity, when combined with intentional collaboration, is the catalyst for high-performing teams.

The Role of Purpose-Driven Collaboration

To create such an environment, Jenna emphasizes the importance of cross-functional teams that self-generate collaboration. These teams are driven by purpose, not just task completion. When people understand the broader picture of how their roles contribute to the company's mission, it transforms their work. "The more each individual gains understanding of other people's roles in the company," Jenna explains, "the greater their awareness of how their function fits into the whole." This mindset shifts the focus from mere baton passing between departments to ensuring the full race is run seamlessly. It fosters a shared sense of responsibility and connection that elevates team performance.

However, achieving this level of unity and collaboration isn't always easy. As Jenna points out, "To create inclusion requires difficult conversations, remembering that each conversation is a pathway toward stronger unity." These discussions often challenge deeply held beliefs, habits, or biases, but they are essential for building trust and mutual respect. Teams must be willing to confront discomfort to break down barriers and build bridges. This requires a heart-centered approach, where every member is respected and valued for their contributions.

One of the greatest obstacles to collaboration is the siloed structure of many organizations. When departments operate in isolation, it stifles creativity and limits the collective potential of the team. Jenna advocates for open discussions, ongoing coaching, and continuous training to break down these silos. Progress demands not just conversations but also actionable steps—feedback loops, training programs, and team-building exercises that reinforce the value of collaboration.

Measuring Success in Diversity and Inclusion

Metrics are another critical component of fostering diversity and collaboration. "Outcomes align with what is measured," Jenna reminds us. If collaboration and inclusion are priorities, organizations must implement tools to track these areas. Measuring cross-departmental communication, team effectiveness, and employee engagement can provide valuable insights into where improvements are needed. Metrics ensure that collaboration isn't just an ideal, but a tangible goal woven into the fabric of the organization.

Ultimately, the journey toward a diverse, inclusive, and high-performing team requires intentionality and persistence. It's about more than policies or surface-level initiatives; it's about embedding these values into the organization's DNA. Leaders play a pivotal role in setting the tone, modeling inclusive behavior, and providing the support their teams need to grow.

As Jenna eloquently puts it, the goal is to create teams that don't just work together but thrive together. By harmonizing diverse personalities and aligning everyone around a shared purpose, organizations can unlock their full potential. When diversity and collaboration are genuinely embraced, they become the alchemy that transforms good teams into extraordinary ones.

A Deep Understanding of Diversity

One of my favorite moments in coaching is when a client has an "aha" moment about a concept we've been working on together. Recently, I had such a moment with a client I'll call "Jerry," a CFO who often expressed frustration about diversity, equity, and inclusion initiatives.

During one session, Jerry said, "I'm tired of this DEI push. Why is it necessary to exclude white males from the workplace?"

I smiled gently and asked, "Jerry, what does your customer base look like?"

He furrowed his brow. "What do you mean?"

"Well," I replied, "are all your customers white males?"

He rolled his eyes. "Of course not. Our product is used by people of all races and genders."

"Interesting," I said, keeping my tone neutral. "Then how do you know what other races and genders need and want if most of your staff are white males?"

Jerry hesitated. "We're not all white males. Okay, maybe the C-Suite is mostly men, but overall, the company is diverse."

"Thank you for clarifying. But my question remains: How do you truly know what your customer base needs when your leadership team doesn't reflect that diversity?"

Jerry stared at me, clearly thinking. "We do a lot of customer surveys. We're always asking our customers what makes them happy."

"That's great," I said. "What percentage of people actually respond to your surveys?"

He looked uncomfortable. "Look, I know what you're getting at, but we're good at sales."

"I'm sure you are," I said warmly. "But let's go back to the question: What percentage of your customers respond to those surveys?"

Jerry sighed. "About 12%."

"Okay," I said. "So, you base your understanding of your customer base on feedback from just 12% of them?"

He rolled his eyes again. "Not entirely. We also analyze our sales data—who buys once, who comes back, and so on."

"Fair enough," I said. "Who creates the surveys?"

"Our sales team," Jerry replied.

"Who else is involved?" I asked.

"Why does that matter?"

"Jerry," I said softly, "because sales isn't just about selling. If you want to create the best surveys, it should be a collaborative, diverse effort that includes other perspectives from across your company. Diversity isn't just

25

about race or gender. It's about diverse thinking—bringing together different experiences and viewpoints to drive innovation and creativity in your company culture."

Jerry was quiet for a moment. Then he said, "I'm just tired of hearing that white males shouldn't be successful."

I paused, letting his words settle. "Jerry, where did you hear that?"

"Well," he said, "there's such a big push for other people to succeed."

"I hear you," I said. "Let me ask you something: Do you see the world through a lens of lack or abundance?"

He looked puzzled. "What does that have to do with anything? I thought we were talking about diversity."

"This is the issue, Jerry. If you think there's only so much success to go around, it's hard to embrace diversity. Let's say you're eating the last slice of pie. Do you believe that's the last pie you'll ever have, or do you trust that there will be more pies to come?"

Jerry raised an eyebrow. "Are we seriously talking about pie now?"

I laughed. "Not exactly. We're talking about mindset. When you live in a mindset of lack, you see opportunities as limited—only so many jobs, so much money, so much success to go around. But when you live in abundance, you trust that there's enough for everyone. Diversity isn't about taking opportunities away from you; it's about creating more opportunities for everyone."

Jerry leaned back in his chair, thoughtful. It was clear the wheels were turning. Sometimes, transformation begins with a single shift in perspective.

He didn't say much more during our session that day, but a few days later, I received a text message from him.

It read: "I like pie. I like eating pie. There's always more pie. I need to shift my thinking."

That simple message brought a smile to my face. When Jerry started to shift his thinking about abundance, his perspective on diversity changed too. He realized it wasn't about limiting opportunities for white males; it was about creating space for more perspectives to be appreciated, seen, and valued.

Over time, Jerry became a vocal advocate for hiring more women and individuals from diverse backgrounds. His new abundant mindset brought him a sense of peace, replacing the resistance he once felt. It also sparked innovation within his company, leading to new ideas and products that boosted sales.

Sometimes, it just takes one moment of clarity to start a ripple effect—one that not only transforms a person but also the culture they help create.

Setting the Stage for Belonging

Diversity initiatives must start at the top, with unequivocal support from senior leadership. Setting aspirational goals, diversifying interview panels, and reassessing job requirements are practical steps toward fostering inclusivity. But diversity cannot stop at representation—it must evolve into true belonging.

A Personal Testament to the Power of Belonging

Kelli Williams, CEO of The Brandlab, illustrates this vital distinction. Reflecting on her career, she shared with me:

"I have often been the only woman and the only Black person in leadership, which meant facing racism and discrimination throughout my career. At one company, despite building a strong, high-performing team that delivered significant results over 2 ½ years, I was still not respected. During a brainstorming session, my boss said to me, 'You don't know what the f** you're talking about. Shut the f*** up.' That was the breaking point. I resigned the next day, vowing never to allow anyone to treat me that way again."

Her story underscores the urgency of moving beyond tokenism toward fostering cultures where every individual feels respected and valued. As Kelli explained, she chose to "create [her] own business—a place where race and gender don't define your value," emphasizing that leaders have a responsibility to empower their teams by recognizing merit and contributions, not surface characteristics.

Building the Pillars of Belonging

How do we cultivate this sense of belonging? It's a pragmatic question, and one that leaders must address head-on. Three cultural characteristics stand out as pillars shaping belonging within a team: character, influence, and trust.

Defining Team and Individual Character

First up: character. Who are we as a team? What's our purpose, our raison d'être? Leaders must engage with our teams to clarify this collective character, understanding the hurdles that may obstruct our mission. Kelli Williams' commitment to fostering an environment where ideas originate from her team exemplifies this principle. By encouraging her employees to "bring any problem to [her]" and guiding them to develop their own solutions, she builds a cohesive team narrative while cultivating individual confidence.

Distributing Influence Equitably

Next, influence comes into play. Who holds sway in decision-making processes? Are diverse voices marginalized, relegated to the fringes of influence? Williams' experience—being silenced despite her significant contributions—reminds us of the consequences of failing to distribute influence equitably. Leaders must grasp these power dynamics and actively dismantle any barriers hindering the equitable distribution of influence within the team.

Establishing Trust as the Foundation

Lastly, trust emerges as the linchpin of belonging. Teams thrive on an environment where members feel safe to express concerns, make mistakes, and share personal stories. Williams' leadership philosophy of fostering support and mutual respect within her team demonstrates how trust transforms work cultures into places of empowerment.

The Path to Excellence

In essence, high-performing teams transcend mere diversity and inclusion; they cultivate cultures of belonging. With a clear sense of character, an equitable influence structure, and a foundation of trust, these teams harness the true potential of diversity, propelling them toward excellence.

Diverse Teams Shine

As the world moves forward and innovation becomes essential, diversity in teams has never been more important. Dr. Valerie Purdie Greenaway of Columbia University has shared unique insights about why diverse teams are so effective. Her research highlights that diversity isn't just a "feel-good" idea—it's the foundation for building teams that excel.

Diverse teams shine in four key areas: starting new ventures, improving existing processes, navigating uncertainty, and responding to crises. They bring fresh perspectives, challenge assumptions, and tackle problems from all angles. When people from different backgrounds come together, their unique ideas create innovation that simply wouldn't happen otherwise.

A Real-World Example: "Mr. and Mr."

A perfect example of this power in action comes from Jemima Bird, who was the Commercial and Operations Director for Moss Bros during the passing of the Same-Sex Marriage Act in the UK. During her interview, Jemima shared with me a story about brainstorming ways to rejuvenate the brand, when two of her team members, both gay, opened up about feeling voiceless but inspired by the new legislation.

Their courage struck a chord with Jemima, and together, they created the bold "Mr. and Mr." marketing campaign, celebrating same-sex relationships. The campaign was a game-changer. It gained attention in Attitude, a prominent LGBTQ+ publication, and even landed Moss Bros a feature in The Financial Times. The effort didn't just elevate the brand's visibility—it sent a powerful message to employees and customers: diversity matters, and everyone deserves to feel valued.

The Science Behind the Success

This story aligns perfectly with Dr. Greenaway's research on how diverse teams work. Diverse perspectives challenge each other in ways that enrich decision-making, creating better outcomes. This process—sometimes called cognitive elaboration—is where innovation really takes off. It's about different viewpoints intersecting, stress-testing ideas, and refining them into something truly remarkable.

Why Inclusivity is Essential

But here's the thing: diversity alone isn't enough. As Jemima's story shows, inclusivity is the key to unlocking diversity's full potential. It's not just about assembling people with different backgrounds—it's about creating an environment where everyone feels safe, valued, and empowered to contribute. For Jemima's team, that inclusivity allowed two voices that might have gone unheard to spark a campaign that transformed the brand and fostered a sense of pride within the company.

The Recipe for Success

Dr. Greenaway's work emphasizes this same principle: diversity only thrives in inclusive environments. Without inclusivity, the potential of diversity remains untapped. Inclusivity is the fertile soil where diverse ideas can grow into meaningful innovation, trust, and success.

When leaders embrace diversity and foster inclusion, they create something truly powerful: a culture where everyone can thrive. And when everyone thrives, the results speak for themselves—in stronger teams, better ideas, and a more connected world.

Breaking Barriers with Compassion

Too often, we forget that at the heart of every team there is the simple need to feel valued and connected. Judging others based on differences—whether it's gender, race, background, or beliefs—doesn't just create barriers; it erodes trust and blocks us from building meaningful relationships. And without trust, even the most skilled teams falter.

A Defining Moment of Exclusion

George Ombado's story is a powerful reminder of how exclusion can hold people back, not just individually but collectively. In 2010, at a Credit Union Conference in Kenya, George witnessed something deeply troubling: women were blatantly told, "You are a woman. Sit down. You should not be speaking." Hearing those words, it's impossible not to feel the weight of how much potential was stifled in that moment—not just for the women silenced, but for the teams and organizations that lost out on their ideas, creativity, and leadership.

George told me that he could have departed feeling disheartened, but instead, it became a catalyst for change.

Leadership Rooted in Empathy

As the CEO of ACCOSCA, George decided to challenge those harmful norms and lead with inclusion. At the time, women made up only 5-10% of the credit union workforce. George knew those numbers weren't just statistics; they represented countless women who had been overlooked, undervalued, or excluded.

By focusing on servant leadership and leading with a pure heart, George began to create pathways for women to rise. He prioritized mentorship, opened up opportunities, and actively worked to foster a culture where women felt empowered to contribute fully. Today, women represent nearly 35% of the credit union workforce—a testament to what's possible when leadership starts with empathy and inclusion.

Moving Beyond Numbers

This story underscores an important truth: diversity isn't just about numbers or checking boxes. It's about creating an environment where everyone feels safe, valued, and supported. When leaders embrace empathy, they transform judgment into understanding, barriers into bridges, and teams into thriving, high-performance cultures.

The Choice of Leadership

We all have a choice. We can let judgment cloud our vision and limit what our teams can achieve, or we can choose kindness, collaboration, and acceptance. When we take the latter path, we unlock the true potential of our people, allowing them—and our organizations—to rise together.

True leadership begins with breaking down barriers. By leading with compassion and inclusion, we not only elevate others—we elevate ourselves and the culture we're building. In doing so, we create something far greater than a high-performing team: we create a place where everyone belongs.

In this chapter, you've discovered practical strategies to build and lead diverse teams. You've learned how to recognize and overcome unconscious biases, create inclusive hiring practices, and foster equity within your organization. These tools will help you transform diversity from a moral imperative into a strategic advantage.

Remember the junior employee whose idea sparked innovation or the manager who embraced discomfort to build a stronger team? These aren't just stories—they're proof that diversity is the winning formula for business growth. When we value and leverage our differences, we unlock extraordinary potential. Diversity isn't just the right thing to do; it's the smartest thing to do, the path to winning in today's ever-changing world.

Winning Takeaways

- Diversity Is a Strategic Advantage: Diverse teams outperform homogeneous ones in innovation, problem-solving, and adapting to change, ultimately driving better business results.
- Beyond Representation to Belonging: True diversity transcends mere demographic representation; it creates environments where everyone feels valued, heard, and empowered to contribute authentically.
- Abundance Mindset Fuels Inclusion: Viewing opportunity through a lens of abundance rather than scarcity helps leaders embrace diversity as creating more success for everyone, not less for any individual group.
- Intentional Collaboration Bridges Differences: Cross-functional teams that understand how their roles connect to the larger mission foster unity across diverse perspectives and break down departmental silos.

- Leadership Sets the Tone: Diversity initiatives must start at the top with unequivocal commitment, consistent modeling of inclusive behaviors, and active dismantling of barriers to equitable influence.
- Metrics Matter for Progress: What gets measured gets improved—implementing tools to track inclusion, collaboration, and belonging ensures these values become embedded in organizational culture.
- Psychological Safety Unlocks Potential: Creating environments where team members feel safe to express concerns, share ideas, and make mistakes is essential for harnessing the full power of diversity.

Winning Success Steps

- Assess Your Team's Diversity Landscape: How diverse is your team across multiple dimensions (not just visible ones)? Where are the gaps in representation, inclusion, or belonging? What unconscious biases might be influencing your hiring or promotion decisions?
- Examine Your Personal Abundance Mindset: Do you view opportunity as limited or expansive? How might your perspective on scarcity versus abundance be affecting your approach to diversity and inclusion initiatives?
- Evaluate Decision-Making Distribution: Who has influence in your team or organization? Whose voices are consistently heard or consistently marginalized? What specific steps can you take to distribute influence more equitably?
- Create Your Belonging Framework: What three concrete actions can you implement in the next month to foster greater belonging among your team members? How will you measure the impact of these actions?
- Design Cross-Functional Collaboration: What opportunities exist to break down silos in your organization? How can you create purposeful collaboration across different departments, perspectives, or expertise areas?

BONUS LEADERSHIP RESOURCES True influence starts with emotional connection. Use these three heart-centered leadership assessments to deepen trust, strengthen loyalty, and lead with both power and vulnerability.

Scan the QR code for your leadership-from-the-heart assessments.

Email me at
sherry@thewinningleadershipcompany.com
to book a **free** 45-minute session.

People don't follow titles. They follow truth.

Chapter 3

Embracing the Hybrid Workforce

Bridging the Gap Between Remote and In-Office Teams

During our coaching session, "Megan," a VP of Operations, sighed heavily and said, "Sherry, I don't think this hybrid model is working. I feel like I'm managing two different teams—one in the office and one remote. There's no cohesion. The in-office folks think the remote workers are slacking off, and the remote team feels left out."

I nodded. "That's a common challenge. What have you tried so far to bridge that gap?"

Megan shifted in her seat. "We've done virtual happy hours and occasional in-office days, but it feels forced. I'm constantly mediating between misunderstandings. I'm starting to think maybe we should just bring everyone back to the office."

"Okay," I said, "let's explore that. What would bringing everyone back to the office accomplish?"

"It would make communication easier, for sure. I'd be able to see who's working and who's not. It's just...easier to manage when I can see them."

I leaned in. "I hear you. And what might you lose by doing that?"

Megan's brow furrowed. "Well, some of my best people took the job because of the flexibility. I'd probably lose them. And the talent pool would shrink if we had to hire locally."

"That's an important insight. So, what I'm hearing is that the hybrid model offers flexibility and access to top talent, but managing it feels challenging. Is that right?"

"Exactly!" Megan said. "It's like I have to choose between talent and control."

"What if it wasn't an either-or choice?" I asked gently. "What if you could create an environment where both remote and in-office teams felt equally engaged and valued?"

Megan sighed. "That sounds ideal, but I don't know how to make it happen."

"Let's imagine it," I suggested. "What would an ideal hybrid work culture look like to you?"

Her eyes brightened. "It would be a place where everyone feels connected—where it doesn't matter if you're remote or in-office. Where meetings include everyone, and communication flows both ways."

"That sounds powerful," I said. "What would need to change to make that vision a reality?"

Megan thought for a moment. "I'd need to create more intentional touchpoints. Maybe rethink meetings so they aren't just for updates but for real collaboration. And I'd need to find ways to celebrate wins that include everyone."

"What might that look like in practice?" I asked.

She started to smile. "We could do team huddles with everyone on the same platform, not just the remote folks dialing into a room of in-office people. We could also set up buddy systems that mix remote and in-office employees to build connections."

I mirrored her energy. "That's a great idea! What impact do you think that might have on your team?"

Megan's face lit up. "It could change everything. If people felt more connected, the misunderstandings might go away. And I wouldn't feel like I'm managing two separate teams. I'd be leading one cohesive unit."

I leaned back and let the moment breathe. "Megan, it sounds like you already have the answers. What's your next step?"

She sat up straighter, a new confidence in her voice. "I'm going to set up a meeting with my team and share this vision. I want to get their input and start implementing these changes right away."

As our session wrapped up, Megan had moved from frustration to empowerment. She left with a clear vision and an action plan, but more importantly, with a mindset shift. She realized that embracing the hybrid workforce wasn't about control—it was about creating a culture of connection and collaboration, no matter where her team members sat.

A few weeks later, Megan sent me an update. Her team was more engaged, and the friction between remote and in-office employees had started to dissolve. It was a reminder that sometimes, all it takes is a shift in perspective to turn a challenge into an opportunity for growth.

The New Era of Connection

In a hybrid or fully remote workforce, the way we build culture has shifted dramatically. Gone are the days when a quick chat at the water cooler or a shared lunch outing could solidify bonds. Today, creating meaningful connections requires intentionality, thoughtfulness, and creativity. It's about more than just setting up a weekly Zoom call—it's about fostering a sense of belonging and mutual respect across digital divides. When teams span time zones and cultural backgrounds, we must address these challenges head-on to create spaces where everyone feels seen and valued.

Imagine a scenario where a team member's day starts while another person's is ending. One person might be sipping their morning coffee while another is tucking their child into bed. This is the reality of global collaboration. The nuances of communication—from email tone to body language on a video call—require us to be acutely aware of how our messages might be received. Building an online culture that thrives begins with this awareness and a deep commitment to inclusiveness.

Small Gestures, Big Impact

One of the most impactful strategies I've witnessed involves incorporating personal touches into virtual interactions. For instance, during team meetings, breakout rooms can be used not for task-oriented discussions, but for something more human. Team members can share photos of recent personal achievements or family moments. This seemingly simple exercise often sparks laughter, warmth, and deeper understanding—reminders that, behind the screen, we're all people with stories, dreams, and lives that matter.

These moments are invaluable. They create emotional connections that transcend job titles or project deadlines. By weaving personal sharing into professional spaces, we remind one another of the shared humanity that underpins our work. Such practices help break down silos and foster empathy, making teams more resilient in the face of challenges.

Food as a Bridge

While virtual interactions are essential, in-person gatherings can add a unique depth to team dynamics. One approach that has consistently proven effective is organizing retreats at a facility with a fully equipped kitchen. These retreats aren't just about workshops and brainstorming sessions; they're about collaboration in its purest form. Each evening, a small group of team members works together to plan, prepare, and serve a meal for everyone.

This might sound simple, but the impact is profound. Preparing a meal together taps into a universal experience. It requires cooperation, creativity, and sometimes a good sense of humor when things don't go as planned. It's in these moments of shared effort—chopping vegetables, debating spices, and setting the table—that bonds are strengthened. People who may have only interacted via email suddenly see each other in a new light, as teammates and friends.

Celebrating Diversity

Food is also a beautiful way to celebrate cultural differences within a team. By inviting members to share dishes from their own backgrounds, we create opportunities for storytelling and learning. A dish isn't just a meal; it's a window into someone's history, values, and traditions. These culinary exchanges deepen respect and appreciation for the diversity that makes a team stronger.

During one retreat, a team member shared a beloved family recipe from their hometown, explaining its significance in their culture. The pride they felt in sharing their heritage was palpable, and the team's enthusiastic participation in preparing and enjoying the dish left everyone feeling more connected. Moments like these remind us that our differences are not barriers but bridges to greater understanding.

The Heart of Hybrid Success

Ultimately, succeeding with a hybrid or remote workforce requires more than just the right tools and technologies. It demands heart. Thoughtful practices like personal sharing and communal cooking create the conditions for trust and camaraderie to flourish. By paying attention to the little things—time zones, communication nuances, and cultural celebrations—leaders can foster a workplace culture that thrives no matter the distance.

The key lies in remembering that culture is not a one-size-fits-all solution. It's a mosaic of intentional actions and shared experiences. When we invest in building connections and embracing the unique contributions of every team member, we create a hybrid workforce that is not only productive but deeply united.

Collaboration Across Continents

The dawn of the hybrid workforce has ushered in unprecedented opportunities and challenges. Leaders now find themselves navigating a world where collaboration crosses time zones, cultures, and communication styles. At the heart of this shift lies the question: how do we unite a team spread across continents? The answer begins with intention and a commitment to connection.

Bryce A. James, CEO of AudiFYZ, outline this insightful approach during our discussion about how to foster a cohesive hybrid team:

"When your team members are in different continents, you must figure out how to collaborate remotely. We do this by:

- Setting clear goals.
- Trusting every team member until they give you a reason not to trust them.
- Doing the right thing at the right time.
- Scheduling follow-ups every week at the same time.
- Eliminating potential anxiety for them.
- Sharing documents.
- Providing projects that people need to work on together."

Setting Clear Goals

Setting clear goals is like providing a map to explorers. Without clarity, teams are left to wander, wasting precious time and energy. One of my former clients, a global marketing director, shared how her team struggled to meet deadlines because everyone interpreted the project differently. It wasn't until she introduced specific objectives, milestones, and a shared understanding of success that her team's productivity skyrocketed. Clarity isn't just about defining tasks—it's about creating alignment, ensuring every team member knows their role and how it contributes to the whole. As Bryce A. James notes, clarity is the foundation of effective collaboration.

Trusting Every Team Member

Trust is the invisible thread that binds remote teams. A client of mine, working in IT leadership, once confessed his initial hesitancy to trust team members he'd never met in person. But when he took a leap of faith, he discovered their capabilities exceeded his expectations. Trust isn't blind; it's built through consistency and communication. When leaders trust their team members, they empower them to take ownership of their work, fostering both accountability and innovation.

Doing the Right Thing at the Right Time

Integrity and timing are the hallmarks of effective leadership. Doing the right thing at the right time might sound simple, but in practice, it requires courage and discernment. I recall a CEO who prioritized transparency during a financial downturn. By addressing his global team promptly and candidly, he earned their respect and solidarity. Making the right choices, even in challenging circumstances, demonstrates commitment to values and people.

Scheduling Consistent Follow-Ups

Weekly follow-ups are the rhythm that keeps hybrid teams synchronized. A sales manager I worked with implemented a system of regular, same-time check-ins, which transformed her scattered team into a cohesive unit. These meetings became a space for celebrating wins, addressing concerns, and reinforcing shared goals. Consistency provides a sense of stability and predictability, especially when navigating the complexities of remote work. Bryce A. James emphasizes that these regular touchpoints are critical for maintaining team alignment.

Eliminating Potential Anxiety

Anxiety often stems from uncertainty. A hybrid team thrives when leaders anticipate and mitigate stressors. I'll never forget a team leader who went above and beyond to provide clarity around upcoming changes. By being proactive, she diffused fears and helped her team stay focused. Small gestures—like being clear about deadlines or providing resources—can alleviate the anxiety that impedes productivity.

Sharing Documents

Shared resources are the backbone of collaboration. Imagine a team where vital information is scattered across platforms. Chaos ensues. One of my clients streamlined her global team's processes by implementing a centralized document-sharing system. This ensured that everyone had access to the same resources, fostering alignment and reducing frustration.

Providing Collaborative Projects

Collaboration isn't just about working together; it's about fostering connection and creativity. One company I worked with discovered that cross-functional projects not only delivered better outcomes but also deepened relationships within their hybrid team. By pairing employees from different regions, they cultivated empathy and understanding, creating a stronger, more unified team.

The hybrid workforce isn't a temporary trend; it's the future of work. By embracing these principles, leaders can turn geographical challenges into opportunities for growth. As you lead your team through the complexities of remote collaboration, remember this: the essence of leadership is connection. When you lead with clarity, trust, and integrity, you inspire your team to thrive, no matter the distance between them.

Finish Stronger Than You Start

During my conversation with Sheldon Stone, Managing Director of Capstone Partners, Sheldon revealed to me his first leap into the unknown, a move to Honolulu fresh out of graduate school. In his first role, he found himself navigating the complexities of collaborating with Japanese clients, a challenge that demanded far more than traditional business acumen. It was here that his philosophy, "finish stronger than you start," began to crystallize. This belief pushed him to not only adapt but to immerse himself fully in the culture, language, and values of his new colleagues. The effort was not about familiarization alone but about fostering genuine connections built on mutual respect and understanding.

Learning Japanese became Sheldon's first step. It wasn't just a practical necessity but a profound act of respect and commitment. Over two years, he transitioned from surface-level communication to a fluency that opened doors to authentic relationships. The transformation wasn't just linguistic; it was deeply personal. By speaking their language, Sheldon communicated that he valued his clients and colleagues enough to invest a significant amount of time and effort into understanding them. It was a tangible demonstration of empathy that resonated powerfully.

Beyond language, Sheldon's journey extended into the cultural heart of his colleagues' lives. He didn't just read about Japan; he went there. He walked the paths leading to Mount Fuji and stood in awe of its majesty, knowing it wasn't just a landmark, but a symbol deeply ingrained in the lives of those he worked with. He listened to their stories about these places, shared in their pride, and made their world a part of his own. These acts of immersion and genuine curiosity led one person to jokingly ask if he had Japanese heritage. It reflected how deeply he had embraced their culture—and how deeply they embraced him in return.

Sheldon's experience offers profound lessons for navigating today's hybrid workforce. Just as he bridged cultural gaps, leaders in diverse and dispersed teams must bridge the gaps of geography, time zones, and work styles. The essence of his approach—empathy, adaptability, and a willingness to learn—is precisely what's needed to foster connection in a world where team members may never share the same physical space. By taking the time to understand and appreciate the unique contexts of each team member, leaders can build relationships that transcend the transactional and become transformational.

In hybrid environments, small acts of connection can have outsized impacts. A leader who takes the time to learn about a team member's cultural background or personal interests demonstrates the same respect Sheldon showed his Japanese colleagues. Whether it's remembering to ask about a holiday they celebrate or adjusting meeting times to accommodate different time zones, these gestures send a powerful message: "You matter, and I see you." This intentionality fosters trust and collaboration, making diverse teams feel like cohesive units.

The principle of "finishing stronger than you start" is especially vital in this context. It's a reminder that building relationships—and maintaining them—is an ongoing process. As teams evolve and grow, so must the leader's efforts to connect, adapt, and support. Just as Sheldon's commitment to understanding his clients deepened over time, leaders must continually strive to understand and uplift their teams. It's not enough to set the tone at the beginning; leaders must sustain and strengthen their connections throughout the journey.

Ultimately, Sheldon's story is about the power of genuine relationships—whether formed in person, across oceans, or through virtual channels. His journey reminds us that success in any environment, but especially in a hybrid one, begins and ends with the human element. By embracing empathy, cultural awareness, and an unwavering commitment to connection, leaders can transform diverse teams into thriving, unified organizations. And in doing so, they'll embody the philosophy that has guided Sheldon to success.

Gaining Connection Through Technology

A similar philosophy guided me during one of my own experiences. As the world shifted toward virtual interactions, I found myself exploring new ways to build and maintain genuine connections—this time through technology. What started as a way to reconnect with old friends turned into a powerful reminder of how intentionality and respect can bridge even the widest of gaps.

Being able to connect with friends, family, and clients from my home office has been an incredible blessing. The ability to communicate in ways that were impossible 15 years ago, coupled with the opportunity to see people as we talk, highlights the importance of maintaining respect in our interactions.

When COVID struck, it triggered a deep need to reconnect with former teammates and friends from my Olympic years. Perhaps it was the fear of the unknown or the stark realization of our fragility as physical beings that motivated this. I decided to organize a 1984 Olympic reunion on Zoom, and 14 of my 15 teammates joined the call. Recognizing the potential for chaos with so many eager voices, I established some structure by preparing questions for everyone to answer. To ensure everyone had the opportunity to share, I directed the flow of conversation by assigning a teammate to respond in turn.

Overcoming Outdated Perceptions in the Workplace

What I didn't anticipate was that my teammates still viewed me through the lens of the person I was in 1984. Back then, I was young, emotionally reactive, and lacked effective communication skills. Anger often fueled my interactions, and my language reflected that with unfiltered curse words peppering my speech.

Today, I am a leadership professional with over 3,800 hours of leadership and personal development training under my belt. Yet, in that Zoom room, my teammates saw me as the 23-year-old version of myself, not the person I've become. This experience served as a stark reminder of how often we view others based on our past perceptions rather than who they are now, which can severely impact communication.

This phenomenon isn't limited to reunion settings. In workplace environments—especially in today's hybrid or remote workspaces—we often hold onto outdated perceptions of our colleagues. A person who once clashed with a coworker years ago may still be seen as difficult or abrasive, even if they've grown since then. Similarly, a team member who started their career as overconfident and disruptive might still be judged by those traits, even if they've matured significantly.

In remote or hybrid work settings, where casual, in-person interactions are fewer, these outdated perceptions can persist. The lack of spontaneous connections—those hallway chats, office parties, or informal collaborations—makes it harder to witness someone's evolution. This can lead to dismissing ideas or innovations from colleagues because we still see them through the lens of their past behaviors. My teammates, for example, treated me as if I was still 23, disregarding the transformation I've undergone, including writing three bestselling books.

Viewing People Through The Lens of Their Growth

The critical question is this: How do we help ourselves and others view team members through the lens of their growth rather than keeping them frozen in time?

First, we must start with awareness. Recognizing that people are capable of change is the foundation. Actively searching for signs of growth and development is the next step. In virtual meetings, where interactions are limited, it's vital to create opportunities to get to know colleagues on a deeper level.

Five Questions for Breakout Chat Rooms

1. What is one significant way you've grown or changed in the past year?
2. What's a skill or strength you've developed that you're most proud of?
3. Can you share a recent success or achievement that might surprise others?
4. What's something you've learned about yourself through remote or hybrid work?
5. How do you prefer to receive recognition or feedback from teammates or leaders?

Recognizing growth in ourselves and others is a cornerstone of fostering meaningful connections and effective collaboration in a hybrid workforce. By shifting our mindset to embrace the potential for change, we create an environment that values personal and professional evolution. When we actively seek to understand our colleagues beyond past perceptions, we unlock their ability to contribute at a higher level and feel valued for who they are today. Whether through structured conversations, intentional efforts to build rapport, or simply offering a fresh perspective, we can ensure that our teams remain dynamic and adaptable. In doing so, we not only enhance communication but also cultivate a culture of respect, trust, and shared success in the ever-evolving workplace.

Winning Takeaways

- Intentionality Is Key: Successful hybrid work environments don't happen by accident; they require deliberate strategies that connect team members across physical and virtual spaces.
- Trust Forms the Foundation: Leaders must extend trust first, empowering remote team members and recognizing their contributions without the need for constant supervision.
- Clarity Creates Cohesion: Clear goals, expectations, and communication protocols are non-negotiable for hybrid teams to operate as a unified whole rather than fragmented parts.
- Personal Connection Matters: Creating space for human connection—through shared experiences, personal stories, or cultural exchanges—transforms distributed teams from colleagues to communities.
- Consistency Builds Security: Regular, predictable touchpoints and follow-ups provide stability and rhythm in the otherwise fluid environment of hybrid work.
- Cultural Awareness Deepens Understanding: Taking time to understand and respect team members' cultural contexts, work styles, and time zones demonstrates genuine care and builds stronger relationships.
- Growth Recognition Fosters Evolution: Seeing team members for who they are today, not who they were yesterday, unlocks potential and encourages continuous personal and professional development.

Winning Success Steps

- Assess Your Hybrid Leadership Approach: How are you currently bridging the gap between in-office and remote team members? What assumptions might you be making about either group that could limit your effectiveness?
- Create Your Connection Strategy: What specific, intentional practices will you implement to foster meaningful relationships among team members regardless of location? How will you ensure these practices are sustainable and authentic?
- Build Your Communication Framework: What systems will you establish to ensure information flows equitably to all team members? How will you make sure remote workers have the same access to knowledge and decision-making as those in the office?
- Design Your Cultural Exchange: What opportunities can you create for team members to share their personal and professional backgrounds? How might you incorporate cultural celebrations or traditions into your team's rhythms?
- Develop Your Growth Recognition Plan: How will you actively look for and acknowledge team members' growth and evolution? What questions or conversations could help reveal the new skills, perspectives, or strengths your colleagues have developed?

BONUS LEADERSHIP RESOURCES True influence starts with emotional connection. Use these three heart-centered leadership assessments to deepen trust, strengthen loyalty, and lead with both power and vulnerability.

Scan the QR code for your leadership-from-the-heart assessments.

Email me at
sherry@thewinningleadershipcompany.com
to book a **free** 45-minute session.

People don't follow titles. They follow truth.

Chapter 4

The Art of Hiring High Performers

Drawing Parallels Between Sports and Business

When I began working with organizations to build high-performing teams, I leaned on my experience as a national championship basketball coach. In sports, success isn't just about raw talent—it's about finding players who thrive under pressure, work seamlessly with teammates, and are committed to continuous growth.

The real challenge in recruiting basketball players was uncovering who the player truly was beneath her skills. While talent was crucial, it became clear that personality traits were far better predictors of success. Champions possess an unrelenting drive, a refusal to give up, a willingness to confront their weaknesses, and the ability to see coaching as an opportunity rather than a critique.

One example that stands out is a player I recruited, "Shelley," who was the most talented athlete I had ever coached. Her moves on the court were beyond anything I could have orchestrated, leaving the coaching staff and the team in awe after many games. She led us to two seasons with 28-plus wins, but when the big games arrived, she didn't show up. The issue wasn't her talent—it was a lapse in her character. Shelley believed her skill alone

49

could carry her through, but when faced with opponents of equal talent, she couldn't confront the possibility of failure. Instead, she self-sabotaged, leaving the team without the player we had relied on all season.

It didn't take long for me to recognize that these same principles are essential in the business world. Some of the most impactful hires aren't those with the most polished resumes but those who bring passion, resilience, and a steadfast commitment to excellence. It's about finding the people who don't just do the work—they elevate the team and inspire others to aim higher.

The Art of Identifying True Potential

I've learned over the years that identifying high performers is an art, not a science. It's about going beyond surface-level qualifications and delving into what truly drives a person. One of my favorite stories is about a young professional I'll call Alex. Alex didn't tick all the traditional boxes for the role, but during our conversation, he shared a story about spearheading a community project that transformed his neighborhood park. The way Alex spoke—with unwavering passion and a clear sense of purpose—reminded me of the athletes I coached who would give their all for the team. Alex joined their organization and became a cornerstone of its success, proving that passion and purpose often outweigh a perfect resume.

Leveraging Networks to Find High Performers

When I'm advising leaders on finding high performers, I encourage them to tap into their networks. Just as a coach relies on scouts and trusted connections to identify top athletes, business leaders can benefit from reaching out to those who understand their mission and values. But it doesn't stop there, leaders must engage directly in the interview process, not as distant observers but as curious listeners. The best candidates aren't just looking for a job—they're looking for a team that shares their values and vision.

The Traits of Exceptional Team Members

Leaders should be attuned to key traits that signal someone is more than a good hire; they're a great fit. These traits include belief in the organization's vision, a focus on adding value, and the ability to adapt and grow. High performers consistently look for ways to elevate the team, just like the most valuable players on a championship roster.

Learners and Leaders: The Ideal Balance

Perhaps most importantly, the best team members are both learners and leaders. They're open to receiving mentorship, but they're also eager to share their knowledge and uplift others. This willingness to exchange ideas fosters a culture of growth and collaboration. Add to that strong teamwork, resourcefulness, and a mindset focused on contributing to the greater good, and you've got someone who's not just a performer but a game-changer.

Building Teams That Exceed Expectations

Helping organizations find high performers isn't just about filling roles; it's about crafting a cohesive and resilient team, much like assembling a winning lineup in sports. By focusing on qualities like passion, purpose, and a commitment to growth, leaders can build teams that don't just meet expectations—they exceed them, thriving together in the face of any challenge.

LaSalle Vaughn's Insights on High Performers

During my interview with LaSalle Vaughn, Chief Compliance, Ethics & Risk Officer at Altruist, I gained invaluable insights into identifying high-performing team members. Vaughn identified five key traits: happy, humble, hungry, fit, and functional. High performers understand that happy people are more successful and maintain a positive outlook on life, bringing a cheerful disposition to their work. Star performers aren't just skilled but uplift everyone around them with their energy and optimism. A happy team member is a motivated team member, and their attitude becomes infectious.

Humility: The Foundation of Growth

Another of Vaughn's vital qualities is humility. High performers are intelligent and capable, yet they don't feel the need to be the smartest person in the room. Instead, they focus on learning and growing. Sometimes people excel not because of their brilliance alone but because they are willing to ask questions, admit when they don't know something, and seek out opportunities to learn from others. This humility can set the tone for the entire team to embrace a culture of continuous improvement.

The Hunger to Succeed

Hunger is another trait that sets high performers apart. Vaughn defines hunger as an insatiable desire to excel and become leaders in their field. Team members stand out who constantly seek feedback, volunteer for challenging projects, and show a relentless drive to grow. Hunger for success inspires other people and raises the bar for the entire team.

The Importance of Team Fit

Fit is just as crucial as skill. High performers seamlessly integrate into a team's culture and align with its mission, enhancing overall cohesion. One person's alignment—or lack thereof—can significantly impact the team's success. When a team member's values don't align, it can lead to a toxic environment where blame takes precedence over problem-solving. In contrast, aligned teams do more than just get along—they are mission-driven and know how to collaborate effectively, ensuring that challenges are met with solutions rather than conflict.

Functionality: Embracing New Challenges

Finally, Vaughn emphasizes that functionality is critical. High performers are those who constantly seek opportunities to expand beyond their current knowledge and skill set. They don't shy away from challenges but embrace them as opportunities for growth. The most valuable team members are not necessarily those with the highest technical expertise from the start, but those who demonstrate a willingness to learn, adapt, and take on new responsibilities. Their ability to evolve makes them indispensable assets to any organization.

Communicating Your Values During the Interview

To attract and retain top talent, it's not enough to create an inspiring work environment—you must also communicate your organization's values clearly from the very first interaction. One of the most critical moments to establish this connection is during the hiring process. Leaders who effectively convey their company's mission, culture, and expectations in interviews can ensure they attract candidates who align with their vision. This became evident when I worked with "Sharina," the COO of a start-up facing a major hiring challenge.

Sharina shared her challenge with me: "We need to hire 50 people in the next two months. How can I find the best of the best for a company that hasn't yet proven itself?"

I asked, "What are you selling?"

Sharina replied, "We sell software that helps companies reward their team members by setting metrics for bonuses."

I clarified, "Oh, I'm sorry. I wasn't asking about your product. I meant, what are you selling to potential team members during the interview process?"

Sharina paused and then said, "Well, we offer comparable salaries and benefits to other start-ups."

I smiled and asked, "If you were the one interviewing for a job and the hiring manager said their salaries and benefits were simply 'comparable,' would that be enough to get you excited about the position?"

Sharina frowned slightly. "Probably not," she admitted.

I continued, "So, what would excite you about working for a company like yours?"

"That's a tough question," Sharina said after thinking for a moment. "I guess I'd want to know about the work environment—things like the company culture, who I'd report to, whether my boss would have my back, if my ideas would matter, and what the company's vision is."

"Exactly," I said. "That's a great starting point. Now the real question is, how do you ask questions during the interview process that communicate those aspects to candidates, so they understand their importance to your company?"

Sharina thought for a moment and then smiled. "Hmm, that's a great question. It's why I hired you. So...?"

"You hired me to coach you, Sharina," I said with a grin. "That means empowering you, not spoon-feeding you answers. The goal is to make your interviews a two-way street—to show candidates how your leadership and company culture inspire your team members so much that they want to be part of your team."

"When you put it that way," she said, nodding, "it makes sense. I need to make sure candidates understand who we are, what our culture is like, and how they'll be treated as team members. They need to know they'll be valued here."

"Exactly," I said. "So, what questions could you ask to communicate that?"

Sharina hesitated. "I don't have an immediate answer. I think I need to spend some time reflecting on that."

"Perfect," I said. "I'll send you some Winning Success Steps to help guide your thinking."

Winning Success Steps are part of my coaching technique where I ask clients to take the time to reflect and think on a deeper level. What I've discovered is that when people write down their thoughts, they are more likely to gain epiphanies that positively transform their careers and lives.

The next time I met with Sharina, she was excited to share her answers with me. She asked, "Did you read my answers?"

"Yes. You rocked the questions. Impressive."

Below are Sharina's answers to the questions I posed:

1. **What are three questions you could ask that would help you understand the interviewees' thoughts on company culture while imprinting upon them the importance of your thoughts around culture?**
   - What type of company culture do you thrive in, and why?
   - Can you share an example of a workplace culture you didn't feel aligned with and how you handled it?

- How do you contribute to building a positive and inclusive team culture?

2. **What are two questions which clarify their expectations of leadership?**
   - Describe the best manager you've worked with. What made them effective?
   - If you felt unsupported by your manager, how would you address that situation?

3. **What are three questions to ask which will help you discover how they value the support of a leader?**
   - In what ways do you expect a leader to 'have your back' during challenging situations?
   - How do you respond when you feel a leader isn't fully supporting you or your ideas?
   - What does trust in leadership mean to you, and how can it be built?

4. **What are two questions that you can ask that will evaluate their need to be heard?**
   - Can you share a time when you presented an idea at work? How was it received, and what did you learn from the experience?
   - What steps do you take to make sure your voice is heard, even in a busy or hierarchical environment?

5. **What are two questions that you can ask that will enable you to determine their alignment with the company's vision?**
   - What role do you think employees play in contributing to a company's long-term vision?
   - If you felt your work wasn't aligned with the company's vision, what steps would you take to address that?

Sharina's thoughtful responses demonstrated her commitment to identifying high performers and aligning them with the company's culture and goals. By using the Winning Success Steps, she learned to connect deeply with potential candidates, ensuring she could uncover not just skills and experience but also values and alignment with the organization's vision.

Sharina successfully recruited team members who fully embraced the company's culture and vision, believing in the organization's dedication to their growth and success. Through this approach, she identified high achievers who propelled the company forward, establishing a solid and distinctive brand identity. This clarity in branding fostered customer loyalty, set the company apart from competitors, and built a strong, recurring client base that fueled consistent growth.

Finding high performers goes beyond reviewing resumes or assessing technical skills; it requires the ability to ask insightful questions that reveal a candidate's core values, thought processes, and alignment with the company's culture and vision. As Sharina discovered, the Winning Success Steps offer a powerful framework to uncover these deeper qualities. By investing time in thoughtful reflection and strategic questioning, leaders can build teams of high performers who are not only skilled but also deeply aligned with the organization's mission, creating a foundation for long-term success.

Lyndon Docherty's Vision for Energized Mondays

Building a team of high performers is about creating an environment where people are genuinely excited to contribute. When leaders prioritize alignment with core values and culture, they lay the groundwork for an engaged, motivated workforce. This philosophy is exemplified by leaders like Lyndon Docherty, who recognized that true success comes not just from hiring the right people, but from fostering a workplace where employees feel inspired and energized every day.

Lyndon Docherty, CEO of HiveMind, during our interview discussed how he envisioned a workplace that defied the dreaded Sunday night feeling—the one where you aren't excited about going back to work on Monday. Instead, he built a company where people feel energized and motivated to start the week. It began with assembling a team of people he genuinely wanted to work with, prioritizing character and compatibility over skills. This approach created a foundation rooted in joy and mutual respect.

Core Values That Drive Success

Docherty's team operates on a set of core values that guide their culture. They believe in appreciating all people as equals and being informed by experience while unified through respect. Their team anchors themselves in humility, reciprocity, and the ability to get along with others. Challenging conventional thinking, they embrace the role of being "Change Mavericks," always looking for fresh perspectives. Most importantly, they prioritize doing what they love, creating a workplace where passion drives performance.

Principles for a Thriving Team Culture

Aligning as a unified team on shared goals is a cornerstone of a thriving team culture. Docherty emphasizes that when everyone on the team is aligned with common objectives, it fosters synergy and minimizes the friction that can arise from competing priorities. Leadership plays a pivotal role in this process by clarifying objectives and ensuring that each team member understands their role in achieving them.

To explore how alignment impacts team dynamics, consider these interview questions:

1. Can you tell me about a time when you worked on a team where everyone was aligned towards a shared goal? How did that feel, and what made it successful?
2. When you join a new team, how do you ensure that your efforts are in sync with the team's objectives?

Think Laterally While Staying Focused on Common Objectives

Lateral thinking involves approaching problems from new angles and finding creative solutions. Docherty's team fosters this by encouraging innovation while staying grounded in the organization's overarching mission. This balance allows for fresh ideas that still serve the greater purpose.

To explore how you approach this during the interview ask:

1. Can you share a situation where you had to come up with a creative solution while still staying aligned with your team's mission? What was the outcome?
2. How do you balance thinking outside the box while ensuring your ideas still align with organizational priorities?

Ensure Purpose-Driven Alignment at All Levels

Purpose-driven alignment ensures that every team member's work ties back to the organization's core mission. This connection helps individuals see the value of their contributions and fosters a sense of belonging. There is often a significant morale boost when leaders begin tying daily tasks to the company's vision.

To examine your strategy for this in an interview, consider asking:

1. What inspires you to connect your daily tasks to a bigger mission or vision? Can you give an example of when this happened?
2. How do you help others on your team see the connection between their work and the organization's goals?

Build the Organization with People You Love Working Beside

Docherty emphasizes the importance of surrounding yourself with colleagues you genuinely enjoy collaborating with. Building a team with shared values and mutual respect makes every project more rewarding and productive.

When navigating this in an interview, pose the questions:

1. Can you describe a time when you worked with a team you truly loved being a part of? What made those relationships so special?
2. What qualities do you look for in teammates or colleagues that make collaboration fulfilling and productive for you?

Embrace Disruption of the Status Quo

Innovation often requires challenging existing norms. Docherty's team thrives by being unafraid to disrupt outdated practices, creating an environment where forward-thinking ideas flourish.

During the interview process, explore this by asking:

1. Have you ever challenged the way things were done in your organization to bring about a positive change? How did you approach it?
2. How do you feel about stepping into situations where you need to disrupt established norms to innovate?

Bringing Together Individuals with Drive and Passion

When you unite people who are deeply committed to a shared vision, their energy becomes contagious, fueling innovation, collaboration, and long-term success. A team of passionate, driven individuals elevate each other, constantly pushing boundaries and reaching new heights. I've seen it time and time again: when passion and drive are at the core, extraordinary results follow.

To gain insight into your approach during interviews, ask:

1. Tell me about a team where the members were passionate and driven. What impact did that have on the team's performance and culture?
2. What does passion look like to you in a work environment, and how do you recognize it in others?

Offer Freedom and Flexibility That Aligns with High-Level Vision

Providing team members with autonomy while maintaining alignment with the organization's goals fosters creativity and ownership. Docherty's team thrives because they balance freedom with a clear focus on their shared vision.

As you conduct interviews, delve into this by posing the questions:

1. How do you thrive when given freedom to work? Can you share an example of when autonomy led to one of your best contributions?
2. How do you balance giving team members flexibility while ensuring their efforts align with the overarching goals?

Always Leave Egos at the Door

Ego can be a significant barrier to collaboration. Docherty's approach to creating a culture of respect and humility ensures that every voice is heard and valued, leading to a more cohesive and innovative team environment.

By doing so, they create an environment where respect and collaboration thrive. Their team's success stems from mutual support, shared vision, and the collective desire to redefine what work feels like. Docherty created a culture where work feels like a passion, not a chore.

When addressing this topic in an interview, try framing the questions as:

1. Can you share a time when you had to set aside your ego for the sake of the team? How did that impact the team's success?
2. What strategies do you use to create an environment where everyone feels valued, regardless of their title or role?

Redefining Mondays for the Better

Docherty's approach to building a high-performing team starts with prioritizing people, cultivating creativity, and fostering a culture of mutual respect and collaboration. By selecting individuals who challenge norms, uplift one another, and bring enthusiasm to their work, his team has redefined what it means to thrive in the workplace. Their success proves that an exceptional culture isn't accidentally shaped; it is intentionally shaped by hiring those who align with the company's vision and values. As a result, they've turned Mondays into a day of excitement rather than obligation, setting a powerful example of what's possible when you hire with intention.

Hiring for Culture First

Hiring the right people isn't just about skills and experience—it's about culture, fit, and mindset. During my conversation with Rich Walker, CEO of Quik!, he emphasized, "We hire for culture first," ensuring that every new team member aligns with the company's values before assessing their technical abilities. By setting clear expectations in job postings and making the application process intentional, Walker weeds out candidates who aren't truly invested in the role, leaving only those who are eager to be part of something bigger than a paycheck.

Filtering Out the Wrong Candidates

Walker's hiring philosophy challenges the traditional approach of casting a wide net and hoping the best candidate surfaces. Instead, his process is designed to attract high performers who are drawn to both the company's mission and its culture. His job postings aren't just a list of responsibilities—they're an invitation to those who seek meaning in their work. By posing questions like, "Have you always wanted to work for a company with a great culture?" and "Do you want your voice to matter?", he forces potential candidates to self-reflect before even applying. This method naturally filters out those who are simply job-hunting versus those who are actively seeking a company where they can thrive.

Making the Application Process a Test

What makes Walker's strategy particularly effective is the final challenge he poses: "Send us a letter explaining why you are the right fit." This simple request does more than just test a candidate's willingness to follow directions—it reveals their ability to articulate why they belong in the organization. Those who fail to include the letter or don't address the prompt are immediately disqualified, reinforcing the idea that getting hired at Quik! is not easy. High performers appreciate a challenge, and by positioning the role as difficult to attain, Walker attracts individuals who are determined, thoughtful, and eager to prove their worth.

The Art of Intentional Hiring

This approach to hiring is an art form—one that prioritizes intentionality over urgency. Instead of hiring out of desperation, Walker ensures that every new team member is a cultural and strategic asset. In today's competitive business landscape, where turnover and disengagement are common, his method serves as a reminder that finding the right people isn't about volume—it's about vision.

Talent Is About Alignment, Not Just Potential

Hiring is about shaping the future of an organization. The most effective leaders understand that bringing in the right people requires more than just assessing skills or past performance; it demands a deeper evaluation of fit, mindset, and long-term potential. This is where the concept of alignment becomes crucial. While intentional hiring ensures a strategic and cultural match, true success comes from recognizing that talent isn't just about potential—it's about finding individuals whose values, motivations, and abilities align with the organization's mission from the start.

Claude Bordeleau, CEO of Vota, shared a powerful insight with me during our interview about hiring that transformed his approach to building high-performing teams. "When I first started hiring, I believed everyone could be 'fixed.' I thought that if I could find the right role for someone and coach them effectively, they would succeed. Over time, I realized this wasn't always true." His evolution in hiring mirrors a lesson many leaders must learn the hard way: talent isn't just about potential— it's about alignment. Hiring isn't about saving people from their own limitations; it's about finding those who are already equipped with the drive, mindset, and passion to excel.

Spotting Red Flags in Candidates

Bordeleau emphasizes the importance of asking thoughtful interview questions and closely observing how candidates respond. He has identified specific red flags that indicate whether someone will truly contribute to a high-performance culture. "Red flags for me include when people take credit for others' work or fail to give credit where it's due. Another warning sign is fake humility—people pretending to downplay their ego while it's clearly driving them." His perspective highlights an essential truth: the best hires don't just bring skill; they bring character, self-awareness, and a genuine ability to collaborate.

Ambition: The Right Kind Matters

At the same time, Bordeleau acknowledges that ambition isn't a flaw—it's a necessary ingredient for success. "I understand that a healthy ego is necessary to build a business. I look for individuals who can confidently admit their ambition—people who want to create value and aren't shy about wanting to share in the success they help create." This philosophy is a game-changer for leaders who fear hiring "ego-driven" individuals. The key, as Bordeleau suggests, is distinguishing between self-serving arrogance and a hunger for collective achievement. When someone openly states that they are okay with the CEO becoming rich as long as they can also share in that prosperity, it signals both honesty and a results-driven mindset.

The Power of Passionate Performers

Bordeleau's perspective on high performers is equally compelling. "The core value of high performers is passion—they must genuinely love to work. Top performers seek out other high performers because they thrive on mutual challenge and inspiration." This is a critical point for hiring managers: skill can be taught, but passion is intrinsic. When leaders build teams composed of individuals who push each other to be better, they cultivate an environment where excellence is the standard, not the exception.

Growth Through Failure: A Hiring Mindset Shift

Perhaps one of the most valuable lessons Bordeleau shares is the role of failure in leadership development. "High-performing teams aren't built by avoiding mistakes but by empowering people to learn from them." He recalls a time when a young micromanager under his leadership made a costly six-figure mistake. Instead of punishing him, Bordeleau saw the experience as a growth opportunity—one that ultimately shaped the individual into a stronger leader. His approach reinforces that hiring high performers isn't just about picking the "perfect" candidate; it's about identifying those who are willing to take responsibility, adapt, and grow. When leaders prioritize these qualities, they don't just build teams—they build cultures of excellence that propel organizations forward.

Beyond Talent: Evaluating Character and Cultural Fit in Hiring

When I was coaching basketball, we spent days, weeks, and months evaluating our recruits. It wasn't enough to watch them play a single game; we needed to see how they responded under different pressures, against different opponents, and in varying circumstances. We assessed their reactions to wins and losses, how they treated their coaches, teammates, and fans, and how they handled adversity. Despite our rigorous evaluation process, we didn't always get it right.

One advantage we had that most companies don't have was the opportunity to meet the parents. Whether children realize it or not, they are often a direct reflection of the values and behaviors instilled by their parents.

One year, after conducting extensive research on a promising recruit, we invited her for a campus visit, thinking we were ready to sign her. However, as soon as I met her parents, red flags appeared. Her father texted throughout our meeting, barely acknowledging our conversation. Her mother interrupted nearly every sentence I spoke. Neither of them expressed gratitude for the tour, the lunch, or the visit. Instead, they spent the entire time complaining—about her high school coach, her teammates, and even the opportunities she had been given.

By the end of the visit, I knew I couldn't take a chance on her. No matter how talented she was, the behaviors and attitudes she had absorbed from her parents would likely carry over into our program. The risks far outweighed the rewards.

The Same Principles Apply To Hiring High Performers In Business

A resume may showcase impressive skills, and an interview may highlight confidence and charisma, but the true test of a candidate lies in their character, work ethic, and adaptability under pressure. High performers aren't just technically proficient—they are team players, solution-oriented, and aligned with the values of the organization. Effective hiring requires looking beyond qualifications and assessing the habits, influences, and mindset a candidate brings to the table. Because in the end, hiring the wrong person—no matter how talented—can cost far more than simply waiting for the right fit.

Winning Takeaways

- **Character Trumps Talent:** The most successful hires are those who possess both skill and character; without strong character, raw talent alone cannot sustain high performance over time.
- **Alignment Over Potential:** Rather than trying to "fix" individuals with the right potential, focus on finding candidates whose values, motivations, and work style naturally align with your organization's mission.
- **Culture Must Come First:** Technical skills can be taught, but cultural fit cannot; prioritize candidates who resonate with your company's values before evaluating their abilities.
- **The Interview Is a Two-Way Street:** Successful hiring isn't just about what candidates can offer you, but what you can offer them; communicate your culture and values clearly during the interview process.
- **Look for the Five H's:** The best performers are Happy (positive outlook), Humble (willing to learn), Hungry (driven to excel), a good Fit (aligns with team culture), and Functional (adaptable to new challenges).
- **Design Your Process to Filter, Not Just Attract:** Create a hiring process that naturally weeds out those who aren't truly invested in your mission, leaving only candidates who are eager to contribute.

- Trust Your Instincts About Red Flags: Small signs of character issues during the interview process often become magnified once a person joins the team; don't ignore these warning signs, no matter how impressive the resume.

Winning Success Steps

- Evaluate Your Current Hiring Process: How effectively does your current hiring approach identify candidates with both the skills and character traits needed for high performance? What aspects could be improved to better assess cultural alignment?
- Identify Your Core Values and Non-Negotiables: What are the three to five most essential values or character traits that define your team culture? What behaviors or attitudes would be considered incompatible with your organization?
- Craft Culture-Focused Interview Questions: Develop a set of questions that reveal a candidate's alignment with your values, not just their technical abilities. How will you determine if they'll enhance your culture rather than simply fit within it?
- Create an Intentional Candidate Experience: How can you design your application process to communicate your values and set clear expectations? What elements could you add that would attract high performers while deterring those who don't align with your vision?
- Build a Multi-Dimensional Assessment Approach: Beyond interviews, what additional methods could you implement to observe candidates in different contexts (e.g., group activities, problem-solving exercises, interactions with various team members)? How will you ensure you're seeing their authentic selves, not just their interview personas?

BONUS LEADERSHIP RESOURCES True influence starts with emotional connection. Use these three heart-centered leadership assessments to deepen trust, strengthen loyalty, and lead with both power and vulnerability.

Scan the QR code for your leadership-from-the-heart assessments.

Email me at
sherry@thewinningleadershipcompany.com
to book a **free** 45-minute session.

People don't follow titles. They follow truth.

Chapter 5

Cultivating the Genius Factor of Your Team

Breaking Comfort, Building Champions: How Discipline Unlocks the Genius Factor in Teams

During my coaching career, both as a basketball coach and a leadership coach, I've discovered a common theme—most people don't recognize their full potential. They settle into what feels comfortable, then plant themselves there, mistaking comfort for mastery. But true growth—true genius—isn't found in comfort. It's found in the delicate dance between pushing beyond perceived limits and having the support to believe you can. That's the art of coaching: knowing when to push until someone feels deeply uncomfortable, then balancing that with empathy. Let them wrestle with the discomfort, allow them to steady themselves, and then push again. If you lean too far into force, they shut down. If you lean too far into softness, they stagnate. The genius of people is unlocked in that space between challenge and compassion.

I learned this lesson firsthand in 1991 when I took over a collegiate basketball program that had been wildly successful—at least on paper. Despite their winning record, the team was anything but cohesive. Their former coach had given them full control, allowing them to dictate their own practices, sub themselves into games, and take whatever shots they pleased. From the outside, their talent masked the chaos. But I knew undisciplined teams crumble under real pressure. When things got tough, when adversity hit, a collection of individuals wouldn't be enough—they needed to become a team.

To complicate matters, the former coach had just moved next door to lead the men's team. And to add another layer of tension, his wife interviewed for my position. The players were loyal to their old coach, and I was stepping into a hornet's nest of divided allegiances and unstructured habits. I had to figure out how to unify them without breaking them.

I started by listening. I met with each player individually, allowing them to share their experiences—the good, the bad, what they loved, what they resented. I never spoke a negative word about their former coach. That wasn't the point. The point was to guide them toward seeing what they needed to become if they truly wanted to win. I laid out the foundation of a high-performing team: trust, a shared goal, productive conflict, discipline, role clarity, and an unshakable commitment to the good of the team over individual desires.

The biggest challenge wasn't pushing them physically; they were elite athletes; they loved being pushed. The real challenge was shifting their mindset, getting them to see beyond their past experiences, beyond what they had always known, and into something greater. The challenge was centered around two star players. Those two star players had always operated with more freedom than the rest of the team, and if that dynamic continued, I would lose the rest of the players. But if I pushed the stars too hard, I would lose them. This wasn't about breaking them down, but about getting them to buy in.

I called a team meeting to define our collective goal. The decision was unanimous: winning a national championship. Every player agreed that discipline was essential. What they didn't realize was that discipline wouldn't just be a word thrown around in a meeting—it was going to become a lived reality.

The first test came quickly. During our first practice, "Mandy"—one of the stars—missed a shot and, in frustration, threw the ball down the court. One of her teammates instinctively turned to retrieve it, but I stopped her.

"No," I said. "Mandy will get that ball. And Mandy won't do that again, or we will all run."

The gym went silent. The entire team held their breath. Everyone's eyes were on Mandy, waiting. She glared at me, defiance in her posture. I didn't move.

"Mandy," I said, "you told me your goal was to win a national championship. Is that still your goal?"

"Yes."

"You agreed with the team that discipline is necessary. Right?"

"Yes."

"Okay, then. How does throwing the ball down the court rate as being disciplined? Does that action help the team or hurt the team?"

"I don't know."

"Let's think about it. If you were in a game and you threw the ball like that after a bad shot or a bad call, what would happen?"

Grudgingly, she muttered, "I'd probably get a technical foul."

I didn't smirk. I didn't gloat. I didn't say another word. I simply stood and waited.

After a long pause, Mandy turned, ran down the court, and retrieved the ball. As she did, her teammates let out their collective breath.

That was the moment the shift began. The moment Mandy—one of the most talented players on the team—realized that talent alone wouldn't be enough. That genius wasn't just about ability; it was about mindset. And when a leader like her started to change, it created a ripple effect. The team began to hold each other accountable, not because they were forced to, but because they saw what was possible when they functioned as a unit. The real genius of a team isn't in individual brilliance—it's in what happens when that brilliance is harnessed toward a greater purpose. That's what turns talent into legacy. That's what unleashes the genius factor.

Creating Alignment for Maximum Impact

If you've ever watched a rowing team slice through the water with perfect synchronization, you've witnessed the power of alignment. Each rower moves in unison, their efforts compounded to create something greater than the sum of their individual strokes. Now, imagine if one rower decided to paddle in the opposite direction. The boat would spin in circles, progress would halt, and frustration would boil over. This is exactly what happens when an organization lacks alignment between the company, the team, and the individual.

To create true alignment, leaders must engage in real conversations—ones that go beyond surface-level check-ins. This means fostering an environment where team members feel safe to voice their concerns, express their aspirations, and clarify how their personal goals align with the company's mission. Too often, organizations dictate rather than discuss, assuming alignment rather than ensuring it. When people feel heard and understood, they are far more likely to commit to a shared vision.

One of the most powerful ways to address misalignment is by confronting conflict directly. In working with a company struggling with internal divisions, I introduced a strategy that encouraged open dialogue rather than avoidance. We designed exercises that placed team members in groups with colleagues they interacted with the least, compelling them to break down barriers and view each other as partners rather than opponents. The transformation happened during structured conversations, where they discovered that their so-called adversaries were simply individuals with different perspectives. By the end of the process, not only had they resolved their conflicts, but they had also built stronger, more trusting relationships.

Alignment isn't a one-time event; it's an ongoing process. It requires leaders to actively listen, mediate differences, and ensure that every team member understands how their role contributes to the broader mission. When this level of clarity is achieved, teams move with precision, innovation flourishes, and the genius factor of each individual is unleashed.

The 15-Idea Rule: Challenging the First Thought

Hobart Birmingham III, RPA, who I interviewed in 2023, developed a powerful approach to problem-solving that challenges conventional thinking—what he calls the 15-Idea Rule. Most people stop thinking the moment they come up with a decent idea. It's human nature—we crave efficiency, and once we land on something that "works," we move on. But Birmingham argues that great leaders don't settle for decent; they push for extraordinary. That's why, in the companies where I've introduced this method, we encourage teams to go beyond their first thought. Instead of accepting the first proposal, we challenge them to generate 15 or more ideas before even beginning to evaluate the best course of action.

At first, this practice can be frustrating. Team members often struggle to push beyond their initial thought process. The first few ideas come easily, but by the time they reach number ten, they're scratching their heads, wondering if they have anything left to give. But as Birmingham emphasizes, this is where the magic happens. By pushing deeper, individuals uncover insights they never would have considered otherwise. It's not about quantity for quantity's sake—it's about stretching their thinking to access untapped brilliance.

Once 15 ideas are on the table, the real work begins. Borrowing from Birmingham's methodology, we put each idea through rigorous evaluation—dissecting assumptions, refining concepts, and identifying the strongest solutions, sharpening the ideas through constructive challenge. The best ideas withstand the pressure, while weaker ones fall away. This process not only strengthens critical thinking but also builds resilience—an essential quality for any high-performing team.

The true beauty of Birmingham's approach is how it fosters a culture of continuous innovation. When team members know their first idea won't be enough, they stop settling for mediocrity. They become more engaged in problem-solving, more willing to take creative risks, and more invested in outcomes. Over time, this practice reshapes how they think in both their professional and personal lives. And that, ultimately, is how we unleash the genius factor in every team member.

The Power of Unlocking Potential

When I was coaching championship basketball teams, I learned that talent alone was never enough. You could have the most skilled players on the court, but if they didn't trust each other, if they didn't believe in the system, or if they felt unseen and undervalued, their performance would suffer. The same is true in business. Your team members need more than just a job description and a paycheck—they need purpose, growth, and recognition.

Defining Roles and Celebrating Shining Moments

Andrew Farrell, SVP & National Sales Manager at Symetra, captured this concept perfectly during our interview when he said, "When building a team with intentionality, it is crucial to define roles and ensure that the members of your team have room to grow and reach their potential. You need to help them realize their 'shining moments' and celebrate their success with them." This isn't just a strategy; it's a leadership philosophy. People don't perform at their best because they're told to. They perform because they feel valued, because they know their leader sees their potential, and because they trust that their success matters.

Leading Through Challenges and Closing the Gaps

But here's the challenge: your team won't always be winning. They will have setbacks, they will face obstacles, and they will experience failures. That's where leadership truly matters. Farrell also reminds us that, "While your team reaches for success, you will also need to lead and coach members of your team through moments where they are challenged and help them close the gaps between the business needs and their ability to get the job done well." High-performance teams are built on a combination of success and resilience when confronted with adversity. Your job as a leader is to create a culture where failures become steppingstones, where challenges aren't roadblocks but rather lessons that propel people forward.

Trust: The Foundation of High-Performing Teams

And here's the key that too many leaders overlook: trust. Teams thrive when there is trust between leaders and team members, between colleagues, and within the very structure of how work gets done. Farrell highlights that "Great teams hold each other accountable, abide by rules of engagement, are vulnerable with one another, and share honest communication." This is the foundation of any high-performing team. Without trust, accountability turns into blame. Without trust, communication becomes guarded. Without trust, people hide their weaknesses instead of seeking help.

Unleashing the Genius Factor in Your Team

So, what does it take to unleash the genius factor in your team? It takes intentional leadership. It takes the courage to acknowledge where your team needs to grow while also celebrating their brilliance. It takes a commitment to recognizing individual "shining moments" while also ensuring that no one is left behind when they struggle. And most importantly, it takes a leader who understands that true success isn't measured in isolated victories but in the collective strength of a team that knows how to rise together.

Advocating for Your Team: The Key to Unlocking Their Genius

Leaders don't wake up in the morning to discover fairy dust has been spread across their teams and now the team is a miracle of collaboration, cooperation, and communication. Leaders champion for their team, advocate for their success, and ensure they understand how their work contributes to the bigger picture. When Robin Daniels, Chief Business and Product Officer at Zensai, and I sat down to discuss this concept, Robin said, "To drive your team's success, it's essential to advocate for them tirelessly. Recognize that their combined input and output determine the company's outcomes."

To unlock your team's potential, focus on their input—values, effort, interactions, and self-presentation—and their output—results in sales, marketing, finance, or HR. By managing both input and output effectively, you influence the outcomes that shape the future of your organization.

Fostering a Culture of Excellence

Your team's success is measured beyond meeting targets; it's about how they show up every day. Are they aligned with the company's values? Are they giving their best effort? Are they fostering positive relationships within the team and with clients? Robin Daniels reminds us that "Your ability to elicit the best from your team shapes your future success. Encourage them to exceed their perceived limits with gentle yet firm support." When leaders push their teams to grow, while simultaneously showing care and investment in their development, they create an environment where people feel valued and inspired to perform at their best.

The Power of Feeling Valued

People don't give their best effort in an environment where they feel like a cog in the machine. They need to know that their contributions matter. Daniels highlights this truth: "People desire to feel valued. If they don't perceive their importance in your vision, mission, and daily objectives, they're unlikely to give their best effort." This is where leadership plays a crucial role—not just in recognizing contributions but in making sure each person understands how their work ties into the company's greater mission. When people see themselves as essential to the company's success, their motivation and engagement skyrocket.

Four Questions That Build Connection and Accountability

To foster this connection, Daniels implements a simple yet powerful practice—weekly check-ins with team leaders using four key questions:

1. How are you doing? (Encourages self-reflection.)
2. What have you achieved this week? (Promotes accountability.)
3. What obstacles are you facing? (Fosters ownership.)
4. Who would you like to commend this week? (Strengthens team connections.)

These questions create a culture of trust and transparency. They allow leaders to gain insight into the team's mindset, identify challenges before they become major roadblocks, and foster a sense of camaraderie by encouraging public recognition of peers. By analyzing patterns in responses, leaders can intervene strategically, ensuring both individual and team goals are met.

The Dangers of Silence: Why Open Communication Matters

One of the biggest threats to a high-performing team is silence. When team members don't feel comfortable speaking up, they create their own narratives, often negative, leading to uncertainty and mistrust. Daniels emphasizes, "Open communication is vital. Without it, people may create their own negative narratives, leading to uncertainty and mistrust." Regular check-ins break down communication barriers and allow leaders to address concerns before they escalate.

A simple yet effective way to open up discussions is by asking, "What are the top challenges you are facing in your role right now?" This question shifts the focus from blame to problem-solving, helping team members feel heard while promoting a culture of collaboration and support.

As Robin Daniels emphasizes, when leaders create an environment of trust, accountability, and open communication, they unlock extraordinary collaboration and commitment. The genius factor isn't hidden—it's activated through leadership that nurtures, challenges, and believes in its people.

Shifting From Blame To Solutions

But sometimes, even with the right questions and a focus on open communication, leaders still struggle to break through team dysfunction. That was exactly the challenge my coaching client, Mya, was facing when she called me in distress.

Mya's voice was tight with frustration. "I don't think I'm the right person to lead this team," she admitted.

I paused, letting her words settle before responding. "What's making you feel that way?"

"There's too much dysfunction," she said, exasperated. "They don't know how to play well together. No one talks to each other directly—they just talk about each other behind their backs."

I nodded, recognizing the familiar struggle. "What have you done so far to address it?"

She groaned. "Everything. I've had one-on-ones with each of them, explained why teamwork matters, and even lectured them about how gossip and backbiting destroy trust."

I smiled. "And how did the lecturing go?"

She sighed. "Nobody likes to be lectured, but they need to hear it."

"Mya, you have three kids, right?"

"Yes," she said, softening. "And they're all teenagers...who have stopped listening to me."

I chuckled. "And what do they do when you lecture them?"

She laughed. "Roll their eyes, give me side-eye, and tell me I don't understand their world."

I let the moment sink in. "So... in other words, nothing changes?"

"Well, not exactly," she admitted. "If anything, they challenge me more. But that's just how teenagers are."

I paused before asking, "Is that really how teenagers are? Or do they just dislike being lectured?"

She hesitated. "It would be easier on my ego if I blamed it on their age, but...yeah, they probably just don't enjoy being told what to do." She sighed. "But if I can't tell them how it is, how do I communicate in a way that gets through?"

I leaned in. "That's the same question you need to ask about your team."

"First, you have to understand why they're gossiping. People gossip when they feel unheard, unimportant, or disconnected. It's a way to vent frustration or regain control in an environment where they don't feel psychologically safe. The real problem isn't gossip—it's that your team doesn't have a better way to express concerns."

Mya nodded. "That makes sense. So, what do I do?"

"Create structured opportunities for open dialogue. One of the most effective ways is by implementing team huddles where people can address frustrations in real time instead of behind closed doors. But the key is to make it a safe space—not a battleground. Try using a 'Clearing Conversation' approach. Have everyone share something they appreciate about a team member, followed by one challenge they'd like to resolve together."

Mya raised an eyebrow. "And they won't just turn that into an excuse to attack each other?"

I shook my head. "Not if you set the right tone. You model it first. You might say something like, 'I really appreciate how hard this team works, but one challenge I see is that we sometimes avoid addressing concerns directly. How can we create a culture where we talk to each other instead of talking about each other?' Then let them discuss. Your job is to facilitate, not dominate."

She considered it. "I like that. It shifts the focus from blame to solutions. What else?"

"Another powerful strategy is implementing a No-Triangulation Rule. This means if someone has an issue with a colleague, they address it directly rather than complaining to a third person. But here's the trick—you have to enforce the rule consistently. The next time someone comes to you gossiping, don't engage. Instead, ask, 'Have you spoken to them about this?' If they say no, encourage them to have that conversation first before bringing it to you."

Mya smirked. "So, I stop being the complaint department?"

"Exactly. And over time, when people realize that gossip leads nowhere, they'll stop doing it. But you have to replace it with a better communication channel. That's why tools like huddles, structured check-ins, and team values agreements are so important."

She leaned back, exhaling. "Okay, this is different. It's not about shutting people down—it's about giving them a better way to communicate."

I nodded. "Exactly. People will always talk. Your job is to give them the right space to do it productively."

She grinned. "I think I can do that."

I smiled back. "And here's the best part—when you create this kind of open culture, you don't just eliminate gossip. You unlock the genius factor in your team."

She tilted her head. "How?"

"Think about it—when people no longer waste energy whispering in the shadows, what happens?"

"They... focus on their work?" she guessed.

"More than that," I said. "They start collaborating. They share ideas freely because they trust each other. They take risks because they're not afraid of being judged or talked about. Instead of hiding their thoughts, they bring their best thinking into the room. That's when real innovation happens. That's when you get problem-solving at a high level, creativity flourishing, and engagement skyrocketing. That's when your team starts operating with collective genius."

Mya exhaled, nodding. "That actually makes so much sense."

I leaned forward. "And the best part? It doesn't take a miracle. It just takes leadership that fosters connection instead of control. When you build an environment where people feel seen, heard, and safe—where they know their ideas will be valued, not torn apart—that's when they do their best work. And that's when your team wins."

She chuckled. "I see what you did there."

I grinned. "Couldn't resist."

The best way to silence gossip isn't through reprimands. It's by creating a culture where it has no oxygen to survive—where direct, open communication becomes the norm, and team members feel heard, valued, and empowered. And when you do that, you don't just eliminate dysfunction—you unleash the genius factor in every single person on your team.

The Three Pillars of Success: People, Processes, and Systems

Success doesn't happen by accident—it is built intentionally, with a strong foundation that supports sustainable growth. During our conversation, Brandon Taylor, Executive Member and CRO Chair at Pavilion, highlighted this by stating, "Success is built on three pillars: people, processes, and systems. Start by hiring the right people and ensuring they align with your processes and systems. This alignment enables your business to scale effectively." Too often, businesses focus on rapid expansion without ensuring that their foundation is solid. True growth means building infrastructure that fosters thriving people, efficient processes, and sustainable systems.

Aligning Individual Aspirations with Organizational Growth

One of the most overlooked aspects of building a high-performing team is ensuring that employees see their personal growth as directly tied to the company's success. Taylor emphasizes the importance of "creating the right culture—one that ties individual career aspirations to the success of the organization." This isn't about vague mission statements or generic development plans; it's about making career progression tangible. Taylor's approach is simple yet powerful: he asks each team member to outline their five-year career plan in bullet points. Then, together, they reverse-engineer the steps required today, next week, and next month to move them toward that vision.

When employees see a clear path for their own growth within the company, they engage at a higher level. They no longer feel like they're just completing tasks; they feel like they are actively building their future. Leaders who embrace this method don't just retain talent; they create a team that is intrinsically motivated to perform at their best.

The Role of Coaching in Unlocking Potential

To bridge the gap between potential and performance, leaders must take on the role of a coach. Taylor points out that "making this vision a reality requires a genuine passion for coaching." This means more than just annual reviews and occasional feedback. It requires a commitment to mentoring, providing both positive and constructive feedback, and helping individuals push past self-imposed limitations. Too often, employees remain stuck—not because they lack ability, but because they lack belief. A great leader doesn't just give instructions; they guide, challenge, and inspire.

Moving Past Excuses and Discovering True Potential

Every leader will encounter employees who hesitate, doubt themselves, or make excuses about why they can't reach the next level. Taylor emphasizes the importance of "guiding individuals to move past their excuses so they can discover their true potential." This requires a balance of empathy and accountability. Leaders must acknowledge their team members' challenges while also refusing to let them settle for less than they are capable of achieving.

When leaders invest in their people with structured processes, strong systems, and intentional coaching, they cultivate an environment where success isn't left to chance. It becomes a predictable outcome—one that benefits both the individuals on the team and the organization as a whole. By focusing on alignment, career growth, and coaching, leaders unleash the genius factor within their teams, creating not just short-term results but long-term impact.

The Power of Genuine Connection

The best leaders understand that leadership goes beyond execution, strategy, and results. They understand that all of those components hinge on people and that people are their biggest asset.

To unleash the genius factor in your team, you must do more than manage them; you must truly know them. When Ruby Deol, COO of AlertEnterprise, and I were discussing that people were the key to every successful organization, Deol said, "You must genuinely love, care for, and understand your people. Get to know their personalities, their families, and even their friends. They need to see that you are both kind and empathetic, while also committed to running a successful business." When employees feel seen and valued beyond their job descriptions, they become more engaged, more loyal, and more willing to go the extra mile.

Intentional Conversations Build Stronger Teams

Building these connections requires intentionality. Deol dedicates time each night to speak with four employees for 20 minutes each, listening to their experiences, both good and bad. "I ask about what's working and what needs to change," she explains. This kind of active listening creates a culture where employees feel safe to share insights, challenges, and ideas that could improve the business. When leaders take the time to understand their people on a deeper level, they create an environment where honesty, trust, and innovation flourish.

Personal Engagement Inspires Peak Performance

Deol's commitment to personally connecting with all 350 employees is a testament to the power of one-on-one engagement. "This one-on-one attention not only helps me gain valuable insights but also motivates them to bring their best selves to work." Employees who feel personally invested in my leadership don't just show up; they contribute with passion and purpose. A thriving workplace is built on relationships. When leaders genuinely care about their people, those people, in turn, care deeply about the mission of the company.

By prioritizing real human connection, leaders unlock a level of dedication and performance that no amount of policy, structure, or incentives can replicate. The genius factor is about creating an environment where people feel inspired, valued, and driven to succeed together.

Winning Takeaways

- True Growth Emerges from Discomfort: High-performing teams develop when leaders create the right balance between pushing people beyond their comfort zones and providing the support they need to believe in their capabilities.
- Alignment Is an Ongoing Process: Creating alignment between individual goals and organizational objectives requires continuous, authentic conversations that help team members see how their personal success ties directly to the company's mission.
- Innovation Requires Going Beyond the First Idea: The 15-Idea Rule challenges teams to push past their initial solutions, creating a culture where people dig deeper to uncover extraordinary insights rather than settling for mediocre first attempts.

- Shining Moments Matter: Leaders must identify, develop, and celebrate individual "shining moments" while also coaching team members through challenges, creating a culture that values both achievement and resilience.
- Structured Communication Prevents Dysfunction: Regular check-ins with thoughtful questions create a culture of transparency and trust, eliminating gossip and transforming negative energy into productive collaboration.
- Success Rests on Three Pillars: Building a high-performing team requires intentional development of people, processes, and systems that work in harmony to support sustainable growth.
- Genuine Connection Drives Exceptional Performance: Leaders who take the time to truly know their people—beyond their job descriptions—inspire a level of loyalty, engagement, and dedication that transforms average teams into exceptional ones.

Winning Success Steps

- Assess Your Team's Growth Zone: Where are team members currently operating—in their comfort zone, growth zone, or panic zone? What specific strategies could you implement to create the optimal level of challenge and support for each individual?
- Design Your Alignment Strategy: How might you create meaningful conversations that help team members see the connection between their personal aspirations and the organization's goals? What specific questions could you ask in one-on-one meetings to deepen this alignment?
- Implement the 15-Idea Rule: What problem or opportunity could benefit from applying the 15-Idea Rule? How will you structure the process to ensure team members push beyond their initial thoughts to discover truly innovative solutions?
- Create Your Communication Framework: Which of the four key check-in questions resonates most with your team's current needs? How will you implement regular check-ins that foster both accountability and psychological safety?
- Develop Your Personal Connection Plan: How will you demonstrate genuine care and interest in your team

members as whole people, not just employees? What specific actions can you take to show that you value their contributions while also investing in their personal growth?

BONUS LEADERSHIP RESOURCES True influence starts with emotional connection. Use these three heart-centered leadership assessments to deepen trust, strengthen loyalty, and lead with both power and vulnerability.

Scan the QR code for your leadership-from-the-heart assessments.

Email me at
sherry@thewinningleadershipcompany.com
to book a **free** 45-minute session.

People don't follow titles. They follow truth.

Chapter 6

The Heartbeat of Leadership:

Cultivating Emotional Connections

From Taskmaster to True Leader

Before the selection of the 1984 Olympic Team, I believed leadership was about wins, the scoreboard, and medals.

In every sport I played—volleyball, basketball, softball, and team handball—I was the setter, the point guard, the pitcher, and the center back. Leadership positions came naturally to me, and I thought leading was about results. I set goals, crushed them, and expected my teammates to do the same. I assumed we were all fueled by the same hunger to win. So, I pushed. Hard. I demanded more, pushed past exhaustion, and only celebrated when the scoreboard confirmed our success.

What I failed to see was the cost of my leadership style. Behind my relentless pursuit were drained faces, uninspired hearts, and teammates who, despite their achievements, felt depleted. I was so focused on the finish line that I never stopped to ask: Was I actually leading, or was I just driving people forward?

It took me too long to realize that success at the expense of my teammates' well-being wasn't leadership. It was a transaction.

The Wake-Up Call: When Success Feels Hollow

There were plenty of moments that could have shattered my illusion of leadership. A teammate walking away from the sport, not because she wasn't good enough but because she had nothing left to give. A once-passionate player going through the motions, playing without joy. Declining performances that weren't due to lack of skill but to emotional exhaustion.

But the moment that truly changed me—the moment that made leadership personal—was when I watched an organization destroy a teammate in the coldest way possible.

Most of us on the U.S. National Team Handball Team had been training together for years. Some had even carried over from the 1980 Olympic Games, which had been boycotted by the U.S. That meant some of my teammates had been training for six or more years, sacrificing careers, relationships, and financial security without compensation. In those days, Olympians were amateurs. We paid for our housing, our food, and our living expenses. The cost of our dreams was steep.

Even though the selection committee had watched us play for years, the final team was chosen through a series of evaluation games against one another. No formal performance reviews. No discussions about strengths or areas for improvement. The only metrics we had were goals scored, and minutes played.

When the selection process concluded, the selection committee gathered all of us into a single room. One by one, they called out the names of the fifteen players who had made the team.

That was it. No preamble. No acknowledgment of the years of sacrifice. Just names.

One of my teammates—a woman who had been with the national team for six years, who had started in numerous games—was left off the list.

The moment her name wasn't called, she collapsed to the floor, screaming. She curled into a ball, sobbing uncontrollably. No one could console her. And those of us who had made the team? We sat in stunned silence. The weight of her devastation smothered any joy we might have felt. There was no celebration, no elation—only the raw, aching realization that something was deeply wrong.

This was my defining moment.

I had spent years believing leadership was about driving performance, but at that moment, I understood that leadership was about people. It's about doing what is right for those you serve. It's about knowing how and when to deliver hard news, about recognizing the emotional weight of decisions, and about treating people with dignity—not as interchangeable parts in pursuit of a goal.

True leadership isn't about pushing people to their limits. It's about lifting them up, understanding their struggles, and making sure that, whether they win or lose, they feel valued.

That day, I saw what happened when leadership lacked heart. And I vowed never to be that kind of leader again.

Breaking Mental Barriers: The Power of Disruption

Leadership is not just about directing people; it's about understanding them. Every person brings a set of beliefs—some that drive them forward, others that hold them back. If we, as leaders, don't help them see those blind spots, they'll keep running in circles, unknowingly limited by the barriers they don't even realize exist. The most powerful leaders I know don't just set goals for their teams; they challenge their teams' thinking. They disrupt patterns, break open possibilities, and create moments of discomfort that lead to transformation. Because here's the truth: if people never feel uncomfortable, they never grow.

Beyond Skillsets: Unlocking True Passion

Of course, leadership is more than breaking limits; it's also about building strengths. I've learned that people's talents aren't always as obvious as they seem. Just because someone is good at spreadsheets doesn't mean they love spreadsheets. Maybe they love organization. Maybe they love problem-solving. Maybe they love patterns. My job isn't to assume; it's to ask. Because when we understand what fuels someone, we can align them with roles that ignite their passion rather than just filling a seat with a skillset.

This is the heartbeat of leadership—understanding that people are more than their tasks, their roles, and their numbers. They are stories waiting to unfold, potential waiting to be unleashed, and brilliance waiting to be seen. When we lead with that in mind, we don't just achieve success— we create it in a way that sustains and uplifts every person involved.

The Heartbeat of Leadership

At the core of great leadership is a fundamental belief in people. During my interview with John "JT" Scott, VP of Enterprise Products & Services at McDonald's, JT articulated this concept beautifully: "I firmly believe that all individuals possess inherent goodness and positive intentions. Embracing this perspective fosters a highly engaged team environment." This belief isn't just an idealistic notion—it's the foundation of leadership that drives engagement, trust, and performance. Leaders who operate with the conviction that their team members want to contribute meaningfully create an atmosphere where innovation thrives, and individuals feel safe to bring their best selves to work.

Eliminating Fear, Unlocking Potential

Fear is the enemy of progress. As Scott emphasizes, "Eliminating fear— particularly the fear of failure and retaliation—empowers team members to innovate freely." When fear dominates a workplace, employees operate from a place of self-preservation rather than creativity. They hesitate to take risks, fearing that missteps will lead to punishment rather than growth. True leadership is about fostering an environment where mistakes are seen as opportunities to learn, not as failures to be punished. When leaders shift the focus from blame to development, they unlock the genius factor within their teams.

Building a Culture of Psychological Safety

Creating a fearless environment requires intentionality. Scott highlights key strategies: "To cultivate a fearless atmosphere, I implement thoughtful planning, conduct rigorous testing, reward risk-taking, and recognize innovative efforts." Leaders must actively shape a culture where individuals feel psychologically safe to contribute ideas without fear of retribution. This means celebrating bold thinking, acknowledging efforts even when they don't yield immediate success, and reinforcing that setbacks are steppingstones to breakthroughs. When leaders champion risk-taking and encourage curiosity, teams respond with energy, passion, and ownership.

Clarity: The Key to Engagement

Clarity is another critical element of leadership. Without it, teams flounder in uncertainty. Scott stresses the importance of clear communication: "As a leader, it's my duty to clearly communicate our purpose, impact, and roles." Leadership isn't about micromanaging tasks but about defining the larger vision and ensuring that each team member understands their role in achieving it. By answering essential questions— such as What value do we offer? and How does our department contribute to the company's success?—leaders empower their teams with a shared purpose. When people understand not just what they do but why it matters, their commitment deepens, and their contributions become more meaningful.

Leadership as the Driving Force

Ultimately, leadership is about connection. The heartbeat of leadership is the ability to inspire, guide, and uplift others. It's about seeing the potential in people, removing barriers that hinder their growth, and creating a culture where they feel valued and motivated. As Scott puts it, "By addressing these questions, we create a transparent and supportive environment where team members feel valued and motivated." When leaders embrace this mindset, they transform workplaces into dynamic, resilient ecosystems where individuals thrive—and where the collective success of the organization is not just a goal but an inevitable outcome.

Beyond the Truck: Leading With Connection

Clay, the CEO of a small company, sent me an urgent text: "I need an emergency call. Now."

Sensing the urgency, I set aside what I was doing and dialed his number. "Hey Clay, talk to me."

His voice was tight with frustration. "I don't know what to do. I think I have a mutiny on my hands. Several of my team members are furious that I bought a company truck and have been using it to drive to and from the office."

I leaned into the conversation. "Interesting. Tell me more about the truck and why your team is upset."

He let out a long sigh. "We needed a truck to visit construction sites. It's a company vehicle, meant to be shared between me and our vice president for site visits. But yes, I also drive it to and from work."

"Okay, so why is your team frustrated?"

His voice grew tense. "One of my employees ambushed me in the hallway. He accused me of buying myself a truck while the team went without bonuses. He said the team should come first."

I let the words settle before asking, "And what do you think about that?"

Clay hesitated. "I do put the team first in so many ways, but I don't think they recognize the things I do. And honestly, I don't want to have to list them out—it feels like bragging."

I nodded, even though he couldn't see me. "Clay, I hear you. You feel like you're already putting your team first, and now you're being called out as if you don't care about them."

"Yes!" he said, frustration laced in his voice. "I've given them raises when I didn't have to. I cover extra costs when budgets get tight. I check in on them, ask about their families. I do so much for them, and yet, here we are."

"Yeah," I said gently. "And how does it feel to hear that they don't see what you do?"

"Honestly? It pisses me off."

I let the words hang in the air for a moment before responding. "I get that. It's painful when you give and give, and it seems like people don't notice. But let me ask you this—do you think this is really about the truck?"

He hesitated. "I don't know. I mean, it might be. But...it feels bigger."

"It is bigger," I said. "Clay, the truck is just the trigger. What's underneath this reaction is a deeper feeling—something emotional that's been brewing within your team for a while. Maybe they feel unseen. Maybe they feel like they don't have a voice. Maybe they're questioning whether you really understand their struggles."

He was silent for a long time. "I never thought about it like that."

"That's the heartbeat of leadership, Clay. It's not just about the decisions you make—it's about how those decisions make people feel. People don't follow a title. They follow someone they trust, someone they feel connected to. And right now, your team is feeling disconnected from you."

He exhaled sharply. "So, what do I do? Apologize? Defend myself?"

I smiled. "Neither. Your job isn't to justify the truck—it's to reconnect with your team. A leader doesn't just explain decisions; they listen. And listening isn't just hearing words—it's hearing emotions, concerns, and even frustrations."

Clay groaned. "I hate these conversations."

"I know. But they're necessary. Set up a team meeting. Not to defend yourself, but to open a dialogue. Say something like, 'I've heard there are some frustrations about the truck, and I want to understand what's behind them. I value each of you, and if there's a gap between us, I want to bridge it.' Then listen. Just listen."

He sighed again, but this time, it felt lighter. "Okay. I can do that. It won't be easy, but I see your point."

I smiled. "Good. Because leadership isn't about being perfect. It's about being present. It's about connecting—not just in good times, but especially in challenging ones. That's how you build trust. That's how you lead from the heart."

He was quiet, then finally said, "Thanks. I needed that."

"That's what I'm here for," I said. "Go have that conversation. And remember, leadership isn't about the truck—it's about the trust."

Cultivating Emotional Connections

The interview with Tarun Gupta, Project Lead and Principal Systems Architect at The Lubrizol Corporation, showed the power of creating emotional bonds that inspire trust and commitment.

"In 1993, I arrived in the United States with just $49 in my pocket and no knowledge of English. My background was in IT, having worked for India's largest company in computer science in 1991. I had been hired by a U.S. company with the promise of a $3,000 monthly salary, and they were supposed to meet me at the airport. But when my plane landed, there was no one waiting for me.

By 10 p.m., a security officer approached me and asked if I needed help. Unable to understand, I could only respond, 'No English.' Hours later, at 11 p.m., the officer found a janitor who spoke Hindi. This janitor, originally from Pakistan, became my unexpected lifeline. By midnight, when my ride still hadn't arrived, he took me to his home despite his wife's protests about hosting a stranger. Out of respect for his wife's concerns, he drove me to a hotel at 3 a.m. and paid for the room himself.

The next morning, he returned to take me to the train station in New Jersey, guiding me onto a train bound for Harrisburg, Pennsylvania. However, without understanding the announcements, I missed my stop and ended up in Lancaster. It was cold, raining, and I was utterly lost. Then, a tall man in a trench coat approached me. Remarkably, he spoke Hindi and offered his help. He explained that he lived in Harrisburg and volunteered to take me there. For the next two days, he let me stay at his apartment.

When I finally arrived at IBM, the location where I was supposed to work, the office was deserted. Standing in the rain at 5:30 p.m., I was approached by a police officer who informed me that I couldn't remain at the building. He offered me shelter at the station, giving me a dry prison jumpsuit, doughnuts, coffee, a blanket, and a heater to keep warm.

Eventually, the contractors who hired me were contacted. They brought me to a one-bedroom apartment shared with five other Indian workers. They paid me $250 a month and covered the apartment rent, but they also confiscated my passport, effectively trapping me. We lived a mile from IBM and walked to work each day. We worked seven days a week, 12 hours a day, surviving on canned beans, boiled eggs, and peanut butter and jelly sandwiches.

On July 4th, in an attempt to celebrate, I bought a pound of chicken. To my surprise, I ran into the same man who had helped me in Lancaster. By sheer coincidence, he lived in the same apartment complex. I shared my situation with him, and he immediately called the police. When the officers arrived, one of them turned out to be the same cop who had given me food and shelter at the police station. That night, they helped us retrieve our passports and gain our freedom.

Looking back on this journey, I am overwhelmed with gratitude for the people who extended kindness to me when I was most vulnerable. These moments of human connection shaped my life's mission: to help others."

Gupta's story reminds us that leadership is about cultivating emotional connections that resonate deeply: the janitor's generosity, the stranger's hospitality, and the officer's empathy are all reminders that true leadership starts with the heart. Leadership is about recognizing the humanity in others and acting with compassion. When leaders demonstrate empathy and emotional intelligence, they build cultures that foster trust, inclusion, and commitment.

The Heartbeat of Leadership in Action

At the core of great leadership is the ability to envision possibilities. Steve Midgley, Atos Group GM, stated during our conversation: "To lead effectively, you must first brainstorm the art of the possible. Set aside rigid execution frameworks initially and focus on what can be achieved." The best leaders don't just dictate strategies—they inspire their teams to imagine, innovate, and stretch beyond their perceived limits. By fostering an open-minded approach, leaders create an environment where potential isn't confined by immediate constraints but instead is expanded through exploration and belief.

From Possibility to Execution

While emotional connections form the foundation of great leadership, they are only the beginning. Once trust and empathy are established, leaders have the opportunity to ignite something even more powerful—possibility. When people feel valued and understood, they become more open to innovation and exploration. It is in this space of emotional safety that leaders can inspire their teams to dream beyond limitations and reimagine what's possible.

Once a leader establishes a compelling vision, the next step is execution. As Midgley notes, "Start by acting on the possible, then empower and delegate to team members capable of handling greater challenges." Empowerment is the key to sustainable leadership. Effective leaders don't micromanage; they build trust by delegating meaningful responsibilities and encouraging team members to take ownership. This approach not only strengthens the team but also instills confidence in individuals, allowing them to rise to the occasion.

Inspiring a Culture of Growth

Stretching a team beyond its comfort zone is what separates good leadership from great leadership. "Once the groundwork is laid, execute a stretch plan—something that excites and motivates your team to grow and create something extraordinary," Midgley explains. Growth happens when leaders challenge their teams to redefine what they believe is possible. However, pushing too far can lead to disengagement. The balance lies in providing motivation while maintaining a realistic and supportive environment. Leaders who help their teams see the benefits of success—both professionally and personally—create a culture where individuals are fully committed to the mission.

The Power of Vision and Momentum

Leadership is about making goals feel real. Midgley shares his "secret sauce": "Visualizing the desired outcome and feeling it as if it has already happened." This mindset fosters confidence and fuels momentum. Communicating a vision with passion and breaking it down into manageable steps allows teams to experience small victories along the way, reinforcing belief in the larger goal. Success isn't an overnight achievement. Success is built through consistent reinforcement, celebration of wins, and continuous learning.

Navigating Challenges with Clarity and Trust

Every leader encounters resistance, setbacks, and internal struggles within a team. Midgley advises returning to the fundamentals: "Stay present. Build and reinforce strategies and the vision. Provide on-the-job training." Trust and transparency are critical in these moments. Leaders must remain accessible, set clear expectations, and ensure team members feel included in the journey. Addressing organizational dynamics—such as lack of engagement, dishonesty, and internal politics—requires a steady hand, an unwavering commitment to the team's success, and a proactive approach to conflict resolution.

Leading with Purpose

Ultimately, as Midgley states, "Leadership is about inspiring belief in what is possible, creating a compelling vision, and guiding your team with clarity, consistency, and trust." When leaders cultivate a sense of shared purpose, they unite their teams in pursuit of extraordinary outcomes. The true heartbeat of leadership lies in the ability to empower others through emotional connection, instill confidence, and navigate challenges with unwavering vision and integrity.

Winning Takeaways

- **People Over Performance**: True leadership prioritizes the humanity of team members over metrics, recognizing that sustainable success comes from uplifting people, not just driving them to achieve.
- **Emotional Intelligence Is Non-Negotiable**: Leaders must develop the capacity to understand how their decisions impact others emotionally, creating space for authentic connection and trust.
- **Fear Stifles Innovation**: Creating psychological safety where team members can take risks without fear of punishment or ridicule is essential for unlocking creativity and engagement.
- **Listen Beyond Words**: Effective leaders tune into the emotional undercurrents of their teams, recognizing that surface-level complaints often mask deeper needs for recognition, belonging, and voice.
- **Clarity Creates Commitment**: When people understand not just what they're doing but why it matters, they bring greater passion and ownership to their work.
- **Discomfort Drives Growth**: The most transformative leaders know when to disrupt patterns and push teams beyond their comfort zones while providing the support needed to navigate that discomfort.
- **Vision Precedes Execution**: Great leadership begins with envisioning possibilities, creating a compelling picture of the future that inspires teams to stretch beyond perceived limitations.

Winning Success Steps

- **Assess Your Leadership Heart**: How well do you balance performance expectations with genuine care for your team members' wellbeing? Where might you be prioritizing results at the expense of relationships?
- **Create Your Connection Strategy**: What specific, intentional practices could you implement to strengthen emotional connections with your team members? How might you demonstrate that you see and value them beyond their contributions to the bottom line?
- **Build Your Psychological Safety Framework**: How can you actively create an environment where team members feel safe to take risks, share ideas, and even fail without fear of retribution? What behaviors might you need to model more consistently?
- **Map Your Communication Clarity**: How clearly do your team members understand the "why" behind their work? What questions could you ask to assess whether they see how their contributions connect to the larger mission?
- **Design Your Growth Disruption Plan**: Where might your team benefit from having their thinking challenged or their patterns disrupted? How can you create productive discomfort that leads to growth while maintaining the trust and support they need?

BONUS LEADERSHIP RESOURCES True influence starts with emotional connection. Use these three heart-centered leadership assessments to deepen trust, strengthen loyalty, and lead with both power and vulnerability.

Scan the QR code for your leadership-from-the-heart assessments.

Email me at
sherry@thewinningleadershipcompany.com
to book a **free** 45-minute session.

People don't follow titles. They follow truth.

Chapter 7

Embracing Uncertainty:

The Dance of Adaptive Leadership

From Control Freak to Flow Master: A Coach's Journey in Embracing Uncertainty

The year was 1993, and I was a young basketball coach about to lead my team into my first—and what turned out to be my only—national championship game. I was locked into routines, holding tightly to my meticulously crafted schedule. I had planned everything down to the minute: when the team ate, our precise arrival time at the gym, the exact length of the pre-game speech—every detail was a piece of my grand strategy.

Looking back, I realized I was a bit of a control freak. I didn't know then that my need for control was simply fear wearing a well-organized disguise. I believed if I could control everything, victory would naturally follow. My mantra might as well have been, "Control the chaos, control the outcome."

But then, of course, things started to go wrong. The restaurant where we had our pre-game meal took too long to serve the food, and when it finally arrived, it was as cold as my expression. One of our vans decided it was the perfect day to play dead. A player showed up two minutes late for the trip to the arena—an almost unforgivable sin in my rigid world. As if to prove that the universe was testing my patience, we hit traffic, throwing off our carefully curated routine by a full thirty minutes.

I was in an out-and-out panic. My assistant coaches, seasoned veterans of my anxiety storms, did their best to keep me from completely unraveling. I was breathing fire, every muscle in my body coiled tight, and yet I tried to mask my anxiety with a forced calm. But emotional energy is like a bad fart—you can't cover it up by pretending it didn't exist. My nerves infected the team. We became rushed, out of sync, letting circumstances dictate our mood.

I tried to fake it. I'd heard the phrase "Fake it until you make it," so I plastered on a smile, but it was as transparent as a dirty window. Luckily, my team was talented enough to overcome my shortcomings. Despite my inability to adapt, they rose to the occasion. They played like superstars, winning the first—and last—national championship for our university in women's basketball.

Fast forward twenty years to a very different version of me. I had learned the art of going with the flow, of surrendering to the moment, and of moving through challenges with grace. I had traded in my rigid routines for a more fluid, adaptable style of leadership.

This time, our game contract for a tournament stated a 6:30 p.m. tip-off. We designed our schedule around that information, allowing the players to sleep in, eat breakfast at their leisure, and enjoy a relaxed early dinner. Confident in our plan, I set off for a morning run.

When I returned, my assistant coach greeted me with news that our game time had been announced as 1:30 p.m. on the local radio. She had double-checked with the university—there was no mistake. It was currently 10:30 a.m., and our players hadn't showered, dressed, or eaten. Under my old mindset, this would have been a disaster.

But instead of spiraling, we adapted. We knocked on the players' doors with a smile and said, "It's time to be flexible and adaptable. Game time is 1:30. Meet in the lobby in 30 minutes. We've got this."

Not a single player panicked. They laughed because the coaches were laughing. They took the change in stride, knowing that their leadership wasn't shaken by the unexpected. We arrived at the gym just 45 minutes before the game, a far cry from our usual two-hour ritual, but the team was ready. They played with ease and confidence, winning the game effortlessly.

The difference between these two stories was a shift in leadership philosophy. In the first story, I was so focused on controlling every variable that I missed the opportunity to lead through the unexpected. By the second story, I learned that true leadership is not about controlling the circumstances but about how you respond when those circumstances change. It is about embracing uncertainty, dancing with the rhythm of change, and guiding your team through the unpredictable with confidence and calm.

Adaptive leaders focus on being present in the now. It's about showing up with a smile, even when the schedule crumbles, and saying with certainty, "We've got this."

Turning Challenges into Opportunities

When I interviewed Karen Halliday, President of NYAK Consulting LLC, I discovered quickly that Karen exemplifies the concept of turning challenges into opportunities. When her company introduced a new incentive and award system based on fact-based, results-oriented criteria, Karen saw an opportunity to rally her team. The submissions required detailed paperwork, and to engage her team, Karen invited their ideas on achieving a 25% improvement in productivity goals. Through daily meetings, tracking progress, and implementing additional training, her team exceeded expectations, achieving a remarkable 40% increase in productivity and saving the company $800,000.

Their accomplishments were submitted to a review panel, and their department emerged as one of the top performers, qualifying for a promised reward trip to Chicago and Canada. However, due to the busy January schedule and the fact that six team members worked on the plant floor, their facility objected to their participation. Despite Karen's efforts to find alternative ways for her team to present their achievements— including submitting a video or presenting on their behalf—her solutions were ignored, and the rules were ultimately changed to disqualify her team.

Standing Up for What's Right

Faced with this injustice, Karen took a bold step. She wrote a formal grievance, sending a detailed letter to the CEO, owner, and relevant decision-makers, outlining the situation and highlighting how the process had been unfair. The next morning, she was called into her boss's office, where she faced the CEO, president, and other senior leaders via conference call. Anticipating backlash, Karen instead presented her case with conviction, asking, "Why would you set people up for success and then not let them succeed?"

Karen's courage paid off. While the outcome of her grievance took time to unfold, her team's response was immediate. They celebrated her willingness to stand up for them, expressing that no one had ever fought for them like that before. "No matter what happens," they told her, "the fact that you stood up for us means everything." This pivotal moment underscored a vital leadership lesson: people lose resilience when they feel their efforts don't matter. Leaders must show that every action counts and inspire their teams to persevere, even in the face of adversity.

The Heart of Adaptive Leadership

Karen's story is a powerful reminder that influence, not authority, is the cornerstone of effective leadership. True change occurs through genuine connection and trust-building. Just as Karen inspired her team by valuing their contributions, leaders who lead with influence create an environment where change is not only accepted but embraced. This principle becomes even more evident when we look at how influence transformed an entire organization, as seen in the story of Mike, a CFO who turned his company around by building relationships and guiding his team toward a shared vision.

Using Influence as the Pathway to Positive Change

Change—it's a word that sends shivers down the spine of even the most seasoned leaders. But let me tell you about Mike, a CFO I coached, who turned his company around using influence rather than authority. When Mike noticed inefficiencies across departments, he didn't storm into meetings demanding compliance. Instead, he started by building relationships. He took the time to listen to department heads, understand their pain points, and empathize with their struggles. By doing so, he cultivated trust, and when it came time to introduce new processes, people rallied behind him, not because they had to, but because they wanted to. Influence is not about power over people; it's about power with people. The only way to make sustainable change happen is by inviting others to the dance, guiding them gently but firmly toward a shared vision.

Influence begins with empathy. When leaders take the time to understand the fears and motivations of their teams, they unlock the key to cooperation. Having a vision isn't enough. You must connect that vision to the needs of those you're leading. Mike helped his team see how their lives would improve with the proposed changes. By aligning his vision with their personal aspirations, he created a shared purpose.

Building influence also requires consistency. Mike didn't just speak about change during formal meetings; he lived it daily. From casual hallway conversations to team updates, he reinforced the message that everyone's input mattered. This consistency established credibility and inspired others to mirror his dedication.

Finally, influence flourishes when leaders are willing to let others take ownership. Mike invited department heads to suggest improvements and take the lead on implementing them. This approach not only lightened his workload but also empowered his team to feel invested in the outcomes. Influence isn't about control; it's about collaboration.

The Only Certainty is Change

Leadership is understanding that you cannot control every variable and learning to move fluidly with the unknown, much like a dance. The leaders who thrive are the ones who embrace change, pivot with it, and turn obstacles into opportunities.

The Strength of the Human Spirit

When Ramesh Jayachandran, EVP/Sr. Technology Executive, Million Mind Corporation, told me the story about his father, goose bumps accumulated down my back. When Ramesh's father, who had contracted polio as a child, spent 43 days in the ICU and endured 20 operations on a single leg, most people would have expected him to break. Instead, his doctor affectionately called him "Mr. Positive"—a testament to his unshakable spirit. He refused to succumb to despair, choosing instead to find strength in adversity. Watching him navigate pain and uncertainty with such resilience became Ramesh's blueprint for leadership. If Ramesh's father could face life's hardest trials with optimism, how could he not do the same in his own journey?

Making the Impossible Possible

One of the most profound lessons Ramesh's father taught him was to challenge limitations. Where others saw walls, Ramesh saw doors waiting to be opened. He refused to let circumstances dictate his potential, and that belief became ingrained in him. As a leader, Ramesh carried this mindset into every challenge—encouraging his teams to think beyond constraints, push past barriers, and turn obstacles into opportunities. Adaptive leadership is about seeing what others don't and daring to act where others hesitate.

Rejecting Victimization and Excuses

Despite his suffering, Ramesh's father never once indulged in self-pity. He didn't ask, "Why me?"—instead, he asked, "What's next?" This unwavering rejection of victimhood shaped Ramesh's leadership philosophy. In the face of uncertainty, leaders can either blame circumstances or take ownership. Ramesh always chosen the latter. Leaders who make excuses surrender their power, while those who take responsibility create momentum, no matter how difficult the path ahead.

Navigating the Unknown with Courage

Ramesh's father understood that uncertainty is not an enemy but an invitation—to learn, adapt, and grow. He approached the unknown not with fear but with curiosity, transforming what he didn't know into something he could master. In business and leadership, we often face situations where the answers are unclear. True leadership does not mean that you have all the answers all the time. Winning leaders have the confidence to take the next step, even when the destination is obscured by fog.

Embracing Change as a Constant

Change is the only certainty in life, yet so many resist it. Ramesh's father, however, embraced change with a steady heart, adapting to new realities with grace. This mindset is critical in leadership. In a world that evolves rapidly, leaders who resist change become obsolete. Those who dance with it, who adjust and pivot with confidence, remain impactful. The ability to embrace change as an ally rather than an adversary is what separates great leaders from stagnant ones.

Inspiring Others to Believe

Winning leaders are capable of navigating through personal uncertainty, and guiding others through it as well. Ramesh's father, in his quiet strength, inspired those around him to believe in their own resilience as has Ramesh done in his leadership roles for the past 20+ years. In leadership, the most powerful thing we can do is instill belief in our teams. When people see that you trust them, they rise to the occasion. When they know you believe in their ability to contribute meaningfully, they unlock a level of commitment and creativity that transforms an organization.

The Legacy of Adaptive Leadership

Ramesh understood his father's life was a masterclass in adaptive leadership. His father showed Ramesh that how we face adversity defines our impact. Within every challenge lies an opportunity to grow, and that the greatest leaders are not those who avoid uncertainty, but those who step into it with courage. The dance of adaptive leadership is about moving forward with trust, even when the music changes.

Adaptive Leadership Tango: A Coaching Story

Ramesh's story beautifully illustrates the essence of adaptive leadership—the ability to move gracefully through uncertainty with courage and trust. This concept isn't just theoretical; it plays out in real-world scenarios every day. One such example came to me in the form of a text message from "Tom," a CEO navigating his own leadership challenges.

My phone buzzed one Tuesday morning with a message from "Tom," the CEO of a fast-growing startup. It read: "Sherry, I think my business is stuck in an episode of 'Survivor.' Help!"

I called him right away. "Hey, Tom, what's going on?"

Tom's voice was a mix of amusement and mild panic. "Sherry, I feel like I'm leading a team of castaways. Every time I think we've built a solid plan, someone shouts, 'Plot twist!' and everything changes. I'm not sure if I'm leading a company or hosting an improv show!"

I chuckled. "Sounds like you're dancing with uncertainty. The question is, are you leading or just trying not to step on its toes?"

He groaned. "I'm definitely stepping on toes. The market shifts, tech changes, and now the new government regulations... I feel like I'm dodging dodgeballs in the dark."

"Okay," I said. "Let's turn on the lights. What's the latest dodgeball that hit you?"

He sighed. "We were all set to launch our new product next month. Then, out of nowhere, our lead developer announced he's moving to a remote island to become a yoga instructor. I mean, who does that?"

"Ah, the classic 'Namaste Curveball.' What did you do next?"

Tom laughed. "I tried to convince him to code from the island. I even suggested he could name yoga poses after our product features. The 'Downward Deploy' or the 'Warrior Bug Fix'—but no luck."

I couldn't help but laugh. "Points for creativity. But seriously, this is a perfect opportunity for adaptive leadership. What's your backup plan?"

He hesitated. "Well, that's the thing. I don't really have one. I keep thinking if I plan hard enough, I can predict everything. But reality is like, 'Hold my beer.'"

"Exactly! You can't predict the unpredictable, but you can prepare to adapt. It's like dancing. You can't choreograph every step in a crowded room, but you can learn to pivot gracefully. What if, instead of seeing uncertainty as an obstacle, you treated it like a dance partner?"

There was a pause. "Okay, so I'm supposed to waltz my way through chaos?"

"Sort of. Instead of rigid plans, set flexible frameworks. When the music changes, you don't freeze—you adjust your steps. Who on your team could step into the developer's role, even temporarily?"

He thought for a moment. "Maybe Sarah. She's been shadowing him for a while, but she's not sure she's ready."

"Great! Then your role as a leader is to guide, not glide. Coach her through it. Help her see that uncertainty is part of growth—not just for the company but for her too."

Tom sighed, but this time with a hint of relief. "I see what you mean. If I keep waiting for certainty, I'll be stuck on pause. But if I move with the uncertainty, I might find a new rhythm."

"Exactly! And remember, adaptive leadership isn't about knowing every step—it's about responding to the beat as it changes. What's your first move?"

He chuckled. "I guess I'll start by talking to Sarah. Maybe I'll even tell her about the yoga island guy to lighten the mood."

"Perfect. And hey, if all else fails, maybe a team yoga session is the answer. Adaptive leadership and flexibility—literally."

Tom laughed. "Alright, Sherry. I'm ready to dance with uncertainty—just as long as it doesn't ask me to do the splits."

"Fair enough! You've got this, Tom."

He hung up sounding more like a leader and less like a contestant on "Survivor." And as it turned out, Sarah rose to the occasion, the product launched on time, and the only island talk from then on was about their upcoming company retreat—where, yes, they planned a yoga session. Adaptive leadership, indeed!

The Realist at the Optimism Party

Adaptive leadership is about creating an environment where resilience and optimism thrive. While Tom's story highlighted how a shift in perspective can transform a team's dynamic, John Gardiner's journey at SOCi, Inc. takes this lesson to a whole new level. Where Tom learned to inspire confidence in his team, John had to blend pragmatism with optimism to steer his company away from the edge of disaster. John shared his story with me which is a powerful reminder that sometimes adaptive leadership means being the realist at the optimism party, grounding visionary ideas with practical solutions.

When John Gardiner joined SOCi, Inc. as CFO, he might as well have walked onto a sinking ship with nothing but a life jacket and a whiteboard marker. It was a turbulent time—tech layoffs loomed like storm clouds, and financial losses were as deep as the Mariana Trench. Despite the chaos, the company was still spending as if it were in the throes of a never-ending boom. It was a bit like watching someone throw a lavish party while the house burned down.

Hope is Not a Strategy

On his 14th day, John found himself in his first board meeting. The room was filled with furrowed brows, crossed arms, and that unique silence only financial uncertainty can bring. When he spoke, he cut through the tension like a hot knife through butter:

"Hope is not a strategy for growth. To turn things around, we need decisive action, starting with cutting 30% from the budget."

If the room had a soundtrack, it would have been a record scratch. Heads turned, and the unspoken question hung in the air: Who brought the realist to the optimism party?

A Three-Step Plan to Dance with Uncertainty

John didn't stop there. He presented three clear strategies, each as bold as it was necessary:

1. Address staff reductions as the final cut. No more drip-drip-drip of layoffs that only fed anxiety and rumors. One decisive cut to stabilize and rebuild trust. Like ripping off a Band-Aid—quick, painful, but ultimately healing.
2. Prioritize employee well-being. Retaining top talent wasn't just a strategy—it was a lifeline. The company invested in travel, training, bonuses, and clear career pathways. They focused on making work not just bearable but meaningful, like adding chocolate chips to an otherwise bland cookie.
3. Transform for relevance. The market was changing, and SOCi had to change with it. John helped launch a comprehensive location strategy, modernize systems, and align budgets with goals. He communicated this vision so clearly that even the office plants felt inspired.

Turning Vision into Victory

The motto that guided them through this uncertainty was simple yet powerful: "We said, we did." They delivered on promises and showcased progress with detailed slides and open communication. It wasn't just corporate transparency—it was like holding a glass house staff meeting, where nothing was hidden.

To reinforce this culture of resilience, John and his team went beyond the spreadsheets. They brought joy and connection back to the workplace. They painted inspiring murals on office walls, threw grand opening events, and celebrated their superstars and all-stars with the kind of enthusiasm usually reserved for lottery winners.

Dancing in the Rain

The transformation was nothing short of remarkable. The team learned how to adapt to the uncertainty and dance with it. And like all great dancers, they learned to trust the rhythm of change, finding their balance even as the music shifted.

John Gardiner's story is a masterclass in adaptive leadership. John embraced the uncertainty, showing that sometimes, the best strategy isn't just to weather the storm but to learn to dance in the rain.

Winning Takeaways

- Control is an Illusion: True leadership isn't about controlling every variable but about how you respond when circumstances inevitably change.
- Influence Trumps Authority: Sustainable change happens through building relationships, understanding motivations, and creating a shared vision that people want to follow, not because they have to.
- Resilience Requires Purpose: Teams develop resilience when they know their efforts matter and when leaders stand up for what's right, even in the face of institutional resistance.
- Adaptability is a Learned Skill: The ability to pivot gracefully comes not from avoiding uncertainty but from embracing it as an opportunity for growth and innovation.
- Reality Must Balance Optimism: Effective leadership sometimes requires being the realist at the optimism party,

bringing pragmatic solutions while maintaining hope and vision.
- Transparency Builds Trust: Clear communication during uncertain times—sharing both challenges and victories—creates psychological safety and strengthens team cohesion.
- Change is the Only Constant: Leaders who embrace change as an ally rather than an adversary remain relevant and impactful in rapidly evolving environments.

Winning Success Steps

- Assess Your Adaptation Abilities: How do you typically respond when plans derail? What triggers your need for control, and how might you reframe these moments as opportunities rather than crises?
- Create Your Influence Strategy: Instead of relying on your title or authority, how might you build connections that inspire voluntary cooperation? What specific steps could you take to understand the motivations and aspirations of your team members?
- Design Your Resilience Framework: What systems or practices could you implement to ensure your team feels their contributions matter, especially during challenging times? How will you stand up for your team when institutional barriers arise?
- Develop Your Uncertainty Dance Steps: What flexible frameworks could replace rigid plans in your leadership approach? How might you prepare your team to pivot gracefully when circumstances change?
- Balance Your Realism with Vision: How can you communicate necessary hard truths while maintaining an inspiring vision of the future? What specific language would help your team embrace both reality and possibility?

BONUS LEADERSHIP RESOURCES True influence starts with emotional connection. Use these three heart-centered leadership assessments to deepen trust, strengthen loyalty, and lead with both power and vulnerability.

Scan the QR code for your leadership-from-the-heart assessments.

Email me at
sherry@thewinningleadershipcompany.com
to book a **free** 45-minute session.

People don't follow titles. They follow truth.

Chapter 8

Driving Change Through Accountability

Accountability is The Pathway Forward

To create meaningful change in your life, there must be a profound moment when you realize that what you're doing is no longer serving you.

At first glance, this might seem like an obvious truth—after all, we never intentionally act against our best interests. And yet, we do. We numb ourselves rather than take accountability for our situations. We find ways to distract from looking inward—gaming, gambling, overeating, scrolling endlessly through social media, drinking, or even exercising to the point of exhaustion.

It's as if we don't want to acknowledge what we already know.

Everything shifts the moment we recognize the common denominator in all our struggles—ourselves. That realization is the key to accountability. It's what allows us to stop playing the victim, reform our behaviors, and rediscover our inner winner.

I know this because I spent decades trapped in a victim mentality. I blamed outside events, people, and circumstances for my reactions. This mindset kept me angry, feeding a deep-seated belief that people were inherently untrustworthy. Imagine being on a team and believing that everyone around you was out to hurt you. Unity is impossible when distrust is the foundation.

The Mirror of Accountability

My moment of reckoning came when I developed chronic pain at the age of 35. I visited 17 different medical professionals, endured countless tests, and still had no answers. After two years of searching, the only solution I was given was to "manage my pain." But I refused to accept that as my fate. Desperate for relief, I turned to alternative medicine.

The therapists at the clinic introduced a radical idea: that physical pain could have emotional and spiritual roots. I scoffed at the suggestion and walked out. But the pain was relentless—I couldn't sit, stand, or walk without agony. Eventually, desperation led me back.

During my sessions, the therapists asked questions about my emotions, probing into my past. I shut down every time. Why dig up old wounds? The past was gone, wasn't it?

Except it wasn't. I had buried my pain, numbed it with alcohol, and convinced myself that ignoring it meant it had disappeared. But the body remembers what the mind refuses to acknowledge.

I resisted. I built imaginary fortresses in my mind—a castle with a moat full of alligators, an army stationed at the top, ready to attack anyone who dared breach my defenses. There was no way I would let my past seep into my present.

And yet, I kept going back. Because despite my resistance, I felt better after each session.

Then one day, my therapist asked me a question that changed everything.

"Can you think of someone who hurt you so deeply that you cannot forgive them?"

I scoffed. "One? Give me a minute, and I'll give you fifty."

She nodded and then asked, "Who is the one person that hurt you the most?"

I inhaled sharply. A tear slid down my cheek.

"Me," I whispered. "It was me."

That was the moment of accountability. The moment I realized that while I couldn't control what had happened to me, I could control how I responded. I saw clearly how my own choices, reactions, and refusal to heal had contributed to my suffering. If I had responded differently in certain situations, the pain I carried might never have escalated. It was a moment of liberation.

From Personal Accountability to Adaptive Leadership

Accountability is the foundation of transformation—not just for individuals, but for teams and organizations. When we take ownership of our actions, we foster an environment where trust, resilience, and collaboration can thrive.

But accountability alone isn't enough. Leadership requires the ability to adapt, to embrace uncertainty, and to recognize that real influence doesn't come from control—it comes from connection. True leaders don't have all the answers, nor do they pretend to. Instead, they create spaces where learning, growth, and shared wisdom become the driving forces of success.

Jason Holland, 2024 Video Commerce Leader of the Year, Firework, shared with me during our interview about how his journey was a testament to the power of adaptive leadership. His story illustrated that resilience is about using challenges as catalysts for growth.

From Control to Crisis: The Breaking Point

Holland grew up in a loving family, yet his all-or-nothing personality led him down a destructive path. Despite having parents who never drank, he turned to drugs and alcohol at an early age, using them as a crutch to navigate life's challenges. As his responsibilities increased, so did his dependence on substances. Like many high-achieving leaders, he convinced himself that sheer force of will was enough to maintain control—until reality proved otherwise.

At 35, he reached a breaking point and made the courageous decision to seek help through a 12-step program. His sponsor asked him a pivotal question:

"Will you let me help you manage your life without question?"

That moment of surrender became his turning point. Holland realized he didn't have to carry the burden alone—asking for help was not a sign of weakness but a pathway to strength. This realization reshaped his approach to leadership, teaching him that true influence comes not from dominance but from shared wisdom and accountability.

Leading with Humility and Authenticity

Getting clean humbled him, forcing him to confront the gaps in his personal and professional life. He learned that leadership is not about projecting an image of invincibility but about fostering trust through authenticity. The same principles that guided his recovery—accountability, humility, and collaboration—became the foundation of his leadership philosophy.

One of the most significant shifts in Holland's leadership style was his willingness to seek input from others. He regularly asks his team members:

"What would you do if you were me?"

This simple yet powerful question creates an environment where every voice is heard and valued. He also acknowledges what he doesn't know, demonstrating that vulnerability is not a weakness but a strength that fosters trust and openness within a team.

Collaboration Over Control

Holland's journey underscores the importance of adaptability in leadership. Rather than positioning himself as the central figure with all the answers, he surrounds himself with exceptional talent, recognizing that great leadership is about collaboration, not control.

He practices empathy, acknowledging the unique challenges and perspectives of those he works with. He also bridges generational gaps, encouraging younger team members to introduce fresh ideas, ensuring that innovation remains at the forefront of his organization.

A key aspect of embracing uncertainty is the willingness to uplift others. Holland ensures that his team members receive recognition for their contributions, reinforcing a culture where brilliance is acknowledged and celebrated. He operates with the mindset that he works for his team, not the other way around. This servant leadership approach fosters trust, engagement, and a shared commitment to success.

The Adaptive Leader's Mindset

Ultimately, Holland's story is a reminder that the most effective leaders are those who embrace uncertainty with courage and adaptability.

Leadership is about creating an environment where growth, innovation, and collaboration can flourish.

Just as personal accountability is the key to self-transformation, team and company accountability are the catalysts for organizational success. Leaders who cultivate these principles set the stage for high-performance cultures, where individuals feel empowered to take ownership, contribute their best ideas, and navigate challenges together.

Driving change through accountability requires the humility to admit where help is needed and the foresight to lift others as we navigate the unpredictable rhythms of change.

From Personal Accountability to Team and Organizational Success

Accountability isn't about blame—it's about ownership. It's the key to transformation. When we stop pointing fingers outward and start looking inward, we reclaim our power. But personal accountability doesn't stop with the individual. It sets the foundation for accountability in teams and entire organizations.

When leaders take ownership of their actions, they create an environment where others feel safe to do the same. When team members hold themselves accountable, trust replaces blame, and collaboration thrives. And when accountability becomes a company-wide standard, cultures shift, productivity rises, and innovation flourishes.

Change begins at the personal level, but its impact ripples outward. True leadership—and true transformation—starts with the courage to look in the mirror and ask, What part do I play in this?

Those Who Are Closest to the Pain are Often Closest to the Solution

Leadership is about connection, purpose, and ownership. When challenges arise, accountability becomes the critical factor that determines whether an organization moves forward or remains stuck. At the core of any discussion in terms of challenges, the fundamental question is: Who takes ownership for the solution?

When I spoke with Gerry Singleton, President and CEO of Montana's Credit Unions, Gerry emphasized this point: "Those who are closest to the pain are often closest to the solution." His words highlight the truth that accountability must be distributed among all leaders, not just a select few. When individuals take responsibility for both challenges and solutions, organizations thrive.

To foster this mindset, Gerry utilized a structured approach that helped leaders clarify their roles and align with the broader mission. This exercise begins with self-reflection:

- What is your edge? What unique value or skill do you bring that no one else offers?
- How does your background inform and enhance your leadership role?
- What is your personal purpose and vision, and how do they align with the team's collective goals?

From there, Gerry shifts the focus to team alignment:

- What is our team's edge? What makes us uniquely capable?
- What are our top initiatives?
- What are our performance metrics?
- What key relationships must we nurture?
- What development opportunities can we leverage?

A crucial part of Gerry's process involves a shared visual exercise. The organization's overarching purpose is placed at the center of the discussion. Each leader writes their personal purpose on a sticky note and attaches it to this central goal. Leaders can connect their personal purpose with the person on their left and right. This act symbolizes how individual contributions support the larger mission and underscores the interdependence of leadership efforts.

Through this exercise, leaders begin to recognize that accountability is not about blame—it is about ownership. When individuals understand their role in the bigger picture, alignment becomes natural, and commitment deepens.

The Power of Ownership

Driving change through accountability requires leaders to step forward—not just when things are going well, but when challenges arise. It demands that individuals recognize their unique contributions and align them with the broader mission. It requires a team to acknowledge their interdependence and commit to a shared purpose.

As you think about your leadership journey, ask yourself:

- What is your edge? What do you bring that no one else does?
- How does your purpose align with the larger mission?
- What role do you play in fostering accountability within your team?

True accountability doesn't come from the top down—it comes from within. When leaders own their impact and align their purpose with the greater good, they drive change that is not just effective but lasting.

The Impact of Ownership: Driving Change Through Accountability

Scaling a company is not about working harder than everybody else in the world; Scaling a company is about working smarter and instilling a culture of ownership at every level. When leaders take full accountability for their actions and decisions, they create an environment where growth becomes inevitable. I once worked with a CEO who was overwhelmed, constantly putting out fires, and never making meaningful progress. He was exhausted, and his company was stuck. When we broke down his leadership approach, we found that he wasn't paying attention to his priorities—he was reacting instead of leading. Once he realigned his daily actions with his true priorities, everything shifted. He stopped micromanaging and started focusing on what only he could do. The business took off.

Think Like an Owner, Not a Specialist

One of the biggest mindset shifts leaders must make is wearing the company hat instead of their specialized hat. Imagine a sales director who only cares about closing deals but ignores product development, or a CFO who obsesses over cost-cutting without understanding the impact on customer experience. When leaders operate in silos, the company fractures. Ownership means looking beyond your department and making decisions that benefit the entire organization. The best leaders understand they cannot think like specialists. They must think like business owners.

Focus on What Only You Can Do

Scaling a business—or a leadership role—requires a clear understanding of your unique value and the willingness to let go of everything else. Consider a high-level executive overwhelmed by daily tasks, a CEO who believed that if she didn't handle everything herself, the company would crumble. But instead of driving progress, she was stifling her team's potential. When she shifted her focus to the high-impact areas only she could influence and delegated the rest, she not only freed herself to lead more effectively but also empowered her employees to step up and thrive.

Own the Problems, Don't Avoid Them

Another key to growth is tackling problems head-on. Too many leaders avoid uncomfortable truths, hoping they'll resolve themselves—but they won't. Weak leadership, poor communication, or broken systems don't disappear with time; they only worsen. Before scaling can happen, these foundational issues must be addressed. Organizations that take an honest look at their challenges, identify root causes, and implement meaningful solutions create the stability needed for sustainable growth. When leaders commit to fixing problems rather than working around them, they set the stage for long-term success.

Prioritize Quality Over Speed

Speed is often mistaken for success, but real success comes from quality. Leaders who push for rapid deployment without addressing foundational issues risk building on quicksand. For example, a tech startup rushed to launch a new product without proper testing, only to face angry customers, massive refunds, and a damaged reputation. They learned the hard way that slowing down to fix problems early prevents costly failures later. True accountability means prioritizing quality over speed.

Break Down Silos and Leverage Technology

Finally, leaders must understand the interconnectedness of departments and fully leverage technology as an enabler. Leaders must recognize that a company is a living ecosystem where every department impacts the others. When communication breaks down, silos form, and teams start pointing fingers—sales blames operations for delays, and operations blames sales for overpromising. The real issue often isn't individual performance but misalignment between departments. By fostering collaboration, aligning processes, and leveraging technology to streamline workflows, organizations eliminate friction and drive efficiency, creating a more cohesive and high-performing workplace.

Commit to Ownership and Watch Your Company Thrive

Ownership is commitment. Leaders who take accountability for their priorities, their teams, and their challenges create companies that thrive. Scaling a business isn't magic; it's a result of disciplined leadership, intentional decisions, and a relentless focus on creating accountability on what truly matters.

Shifting Accountability From Blame to Opportunity

When accountability is embraced, it transforms businesses. But what happens when accountability is missing? When deadlines slip, and excuses multiply, leaders are left spinning their wheels. The truth is accountability isn't just about assigning blame—it's about creating opportunities for growth and alignment. When "Jenna," the COO of a mid-sized tech company, reached out to me, it became clear just how critical this shift can be.

My phone buzzed with a text from Jenna, the COO of a mid-sized tech company, "Sherry, I need an accountability intervention. Stat!"

I called her immediately. "Hey Jenna, what's going on?"

She answered with a mix of exasperation and defeat. "I think my team is allergic to accountability. Every deadline is a moving target. It's like playing whack-a-mole with excuses."

I chuckled. "I get it. Sometimes it feels like the Accountability Fairy needs a bigger wand. What's the latest mole that popped up?"

121

She sighed. "We had a project due last Friday. Everyone agreed on the timeline, but when I checked in, only half the tasks were done. When I asked why, I got a symphony of reasons—sick kids, lost emails, a dog that apparently ate not just homework but entire project files."

I couldn't help but laugh. "That's one talented dog. So, what did you do next?"

"I told them we needed to get it done ASAP, but it turned into a blame game. 'I thought Mark was doing it,' 'Oh, I was waiting for Sarah,' 'I didn't realize we had a deadline.' It was like a bad reality show."

I nodded. "Sounds like accountability is slipping through the cracks. When you set the deadline, how clear were roles and responsibilities?"

Jenna hesitated. "Well, I thought I was clear. I said, 'We need this by Friday,' and everyone nodded. I took that as confirmation."

"Ah, the classic 'nod of doom,'" I said. "Nodding is like the universal sign for 'I'm not really listening, but I want this meeting to end.'"

She snorted. "Exactly! So, what do I do? I don't want to micromanage, but I also can't keep pulling rabbits out of hats to meet deadlines."

"Totally. You shouldn't have to become the Accountability Police. But maybe the issue isn't enforcement—it's clarity. How do you typically assign tasks?"

"Usually, I outline what needs to be done and ask if everyone's on board. Then I trust them to handle it."

"Trust is great, but trust without clarity leads to chaos. What if instead of asking if everyone's on board, you assign specific tasks with clear deadlines and ask each person to verbally commit?"

Jenna paused. "You mean make them say it out loud? Like, 'I, Mark, solemnly swear to complete my task'?"

"Exactly—minus the Hogwarts vibe. When people say it out loud, it reinforces commitment. Plus, it eliminates the 'I thought someone else was doing it' excuse."

She let out a breath. "Okay, I can try that. And what about when they still miss deadlines? I hate feeling like the bad guy."

"Here's the thing, Jenna: Accountability isn't about being the bad leader—it's about being the consistent leader. It's not about catching people out but helping them step up. When someone misses a deadline, shift the conversation from 'Why didn't you?' to 'What got in the way?' and 'How can we fix this together?'"

Her voice lightened. "I like that. It feels less confrontational and more supportive. But what if they keep dropping the ball?"

"Then it's time for the 'Repeat Offender' chat. Be direct but kind. 'Jenna, I've noticed a pattern. You've missed three deadlines this month. What's going on, and how can I support you in meeting expectations?' It's not about blame—it's about opening the door to honesty and growth."

She was quiet for a moment. "You know, I've been avoiding those conversations because I didn't want to seem harsh. But now I see that avoiding them is actually enabling the problem."

"Exactly. Accountability isn't a punishment—it's a gift. It gives your team the structure they need to thrive. And when they know you'll follow through, it builds trust. People want to be held accountable—it shows you believe in their potential."

Jenna laughed. "Okay, Sherry, I'll put on my Accountability Cape. Maybe not a full cape—just a stylish blazer. But I'll do it."

I grinned. "Perfect. And remember, accountability isn't about control—it's about creating a culture where promises are kept, and growth is real. You've got this."

"Thanks, Sherry. I needed that."

"Anytime. Go sprinkle some accountability magic on that team—and maybe keep the dog away from the project files this time."

She hung up with a lighter tone, ready to lead with both clarity and a dash of humor.

Building Leadership on a Foundation of Character

Jenna's story is a testament to how a shift in mindset can transform a team's accountability. But true leadership goes even deeper—it starts with character. Leaders who build their organizations on a foundation of integrity and purpose create a culture where accountability is embraced. Sanjeev Kumar, CEO of Eficens Systems, exemplifies this kind of leadership, rooted in values that guide not only his decisions but also the hearts and minds of his team.

Sanjeev told me during our interview that he attributed his leadership philosophy to an early education rooted in character development. Growing up in India, he attended an isolated school, located 100 miles from the nearest bustling town. While academics played a role, the true focus was on shaping values like integrity, resilience, and compassion. These principles became the foundation of his leadership, guiding how he builds teams, fosters accountability, and shapes organizational cultures.

For Kumar, leadership is about instilling a deep sense of purpose. When team members feel connected to something greater than themselves, they are naturally driven to take ownership of their work. This intrinsic motivation fuels accountability, not through external pressure, but through personal investment in outcomes.

Accountability: A Byproduct of Purpose and Trust

Kumar believes that accountability isn't achieved through force or fear. Instead, it flourishes in an environment where individuals recognize their potential and understand how their contributions impact the bigger picture. When employees are empowered to create and innovate, they develop a stronger commitment to the success of the organization.

However, fostering this level of accountability requires intention. Leaders must not only communicate expectations but also create a culture where people feel supported in their growth. When employees trust that leadership is invested in their success, accountability becomes an organic byproduct of alignment and purpose. But to sustain this, a clearly defined culture code is essential—one that outlines the values and behaviors expected from everyone.

The Five Core Principles of an Accountable Culture

In his leadership journey, Kumar has identified five core principles that drive both accountability and innovation within his teams:

1. Influence courageously – Lead with boldness and inspire others to act.
2. Collaborate abundantly – Embrace teamwork as the foundation for success.
3. Share your knowledge and ideas – Ensure the free flow of information to spark growth.
4. Speak freely – Break down hierarchical barriers to create an environment of open communication.
5. Act boldly – Take calculated risks and foster innovation at deeper levels.

When leaders consistently uphold these values, they create an environment where accountability is not an obligation but a natural result of shared vision and empowerment. Employees feel a greater sense of ownership and are inspired to contribute at their highest level.

Shifting from Control to Ownership

Too often, leaders attempt to drive accountability through strict oversight and rigid policies. But Kumar's experience has shown that true accountability comes from within—it cannot be enforced; it must be cultivated. People who feel valued and trusted are more likely to take responsibility for their actions, while those operating under fear tend to disengage or deflect blame.

This shift from control to ownership transforms not just individual performance but entire teams and organizations. Leaders who focus on building trust and alignment rather than micromanaging create cultures where accountability thrives effortlessly.

The Path to Lasting Change

The result of this leadership approach is a workplace where people feel seen, supported, and inspired to give their best. When leaders foster an environment that prioritizes purpose, trust, and shared responsibility, accountability becomes second nature.

"This is how true change is driven," says Kumar. "Not through control, but through ownership and purpose."

By defining core values, empowering individuals, and leading with authenticity, leaders can create a culture where accountability and innovation flourish—ensuring sustainable success for both people and the organization.

Winning Takeaways

- **Self-Accountability Precedes Organizational Accountability:** Transformative leadership begins with the courage to look inward and acknowledge your own role in both successes and failures.
- **Ownership Is Liberation, Not Burden:** Taking accountability isn't about blame or punishment—it's about reclaiming your power to initiate change and create solutions.
- **Clarity Is the Foundation of Commitment:** Clear expectations, specific responsibilities, and verbal confirmation create the structure needed for accountability to flourish.
- **From Blame to Solution:** Shifting accountability conversations from "Why didn't you?" to "What got in the way?" and "How can we fix this together?" transforms criticism into collaboration.
- **Those Closest to the Pain Are Closest to the Solution:** Distributing accountability throughout the organization empowers those with direct experience to create the most effective solutions.
- **Think Like an Owner, Not a Specialist:** Breaking down silos and considering whole-organization impact creates leadership that transcends departmental boundaries.
- **Purpose Fuels Accountability:** When team members connect their work to a meaningful purpose and understand how their contributions impact the bigger picture, accountability becomes intrinsic rather than imposed.

Winning Success Steps

- Conduct Your Personal Accountability Audit: Where in your leadership are you pointing fingers outward rather than looking inward? What challenge or struggle could transform if you asked, "What part do I play in this?"
- Identify Your Leadership Edge: What unique value do you bring that no one else offers? How does this edge align with your personal purpose and the broader mission of your organization?
- Create Your Clarity Framework: How can you improve the clarity of expectations, roles, and deadlines in your team? What specific verbal commitment practices could you implement to strengthen accountability?
- Design Your Solution-Focused Approach: How might you reframe accountability conversations to focus on solutions rather than blame? What questions could you ask that open doors to honesty and growth?
- Develop Your Ownership Culture Plan: What specific actions could you take to shift your organization from control to ownership? How will you create an environment where accountability is cultivated through purpose and trust rather than enforced through policies?

BONUS LEADERSHIP RESOURCES True influence starts with emotional connection. Use these three heart-centered leadership assessments to deepen trust, strengthen loyalty, and lead with both power and vulnerability.

Scan the QR code for your leadership-from-the-heart assessments.

Email me at
sherry@thewinningleadershipcompany.com
to book a **free** 45-minute session.

People don't follow titles. They follow truth.

Chapter 9

The Leader's Journey - From Winning Games to Winning Hearts

The Leadership Dance Recital

We've come a long way together, haven't we? From discovering your Leadership North Star to embracing accountability, we've covered quite the dance floor. If this book were a dance recital, you'd have learned the waltz of vision, the tango of diversity, the freestyle of hybrid leadership, the precise choreography of hiring high performers, the jazz improvisation of cultivating genius, the heartfelt ballet of emotional connection, the swing of adaptability, and the steady rhythm of accountability.

That's a lot of dancing—and probably explains why your mental feet are tired.

But here's the truth about leadership that most books won't tell you: you're never finished learning. Just when you think you've mastered the foxtrot of strategic planning, someone changes the music to hip-hop, and you're standing there wondering what happened to the nice, predictable beat you were counting on.

And that's exactly as it should be.

The Unfinished Symphony of Leadership

If there's one message I want you to take from this book, it's this: great leadership isn't a destination—it's a journey. It's not about reaching some mythical state of leadership perfection where your team never struggles, your decisions are always right, and your hair always looks amazing in Zoom meetings. (Though if you've figured out that last one, please call me immediately.)

Leadership is messy because humans are complex, business is unpredictable, and life has a way of throwing curveballs when you're expecting fastballs. The leaders who truly excel aren't the ones who avoid difficulties—they're the ones who navigate them with grace, authenticity, and a healthy dose of humility.

Remember Jason Holland's journey from addiction to adaptive leadership? Or John Gardiner's courageous realism that saved a company teetering on the brink? These leaders didn't succeed because they had all the answers. They succeeded because they were willing to ask better questions, to challenge their own assumptions, and to put connection above control.

The Greatest Leadership Secret (That Isn't Really a Secret)

Throughout this book, we've explored different dimensions of high-performance leadership, but they all circle back to one central truth: leadership isn't about you—it's about the people you serve.

Yes, you need a clear vision. Yes, you need to embrace diversity and build resilient teams. Yes, you need frameworks for hiring, developing talent, adapting to change, and fostering accountability. But all of these tools are meaningless if they're not built on a foundation of genuine care for the people you lead.

I learned this lesson the hard way, standing in that Olympic team selection room, watching my teammate collapse in anguish because the system treated her as disposable after years of sacrifice. I learned it again as a basketball coach, when my rigid control masked my fear and nearly cost us a championship. And I've seen it play out in boardrooms and executive suites around the world—leaders who focus on metrics at the expense of meaning, who prioritize schedules over people, and who wonder why their brilliant strategies fall flat in execution.

The secret? People follow leaders who see them—truly see them—as human beings first and resources second.

Your Leadership Playlist: Greatest Hits from the Chapters

As we wrap up our journey together, let's revisit some of the most powerful insights from each chapter—think of it as your leadership playlist for the road ahead:

From Chapter 1: The Leadership North Star

True north isn't just about knowing where you're going; it's about bringing others along willingly. Your vision is only as powerful as your ability to connect it to the aspirations of those you lead.

From Chapter 2: Diversity: The Alchemy of a High-Performance Team

Diversity isn't about checking boxes; it's about creating the conditions where different perspectives can blend into something greater than the sum of their parts. The magic happens when every voice matters and everyone knows it.

From Chapter 3: Embracing the Hybrid Workforce

Distance is a challenge, not an excuse. When you can't rely on physical proximity, you must double down on intentional connection, clear communication, and cultural touchpoints that transcend geography.

From Chapter 4: The Art of Hiring High Performers

Hiring is destiny. The brilliance of your strategy means nothing if your team lacks the character, competence, and cultural alignment to execute it. Hire people who elevate your organization, not just fill seats.

From Chapter 5: Cultivating the Genius Factor of Your Team

Genius isn't rare—it's just rarely activated. Your job isn't to be the smartest person in the room; it's to create conditions where everyone's intelligence and creativity can flourish without fear.

From Chapter 6: The Heartbeat of Leadership

Emotional connection isn't soft—it's the hardest and most essential work of leadership. When Clay realized his team's reaction to the truck wasn't about the vehicle but about feeling valued, he discovered the true currency of leadership: trust.

From Chapter 7: Embracing Uncertainty

The leaders who thrive aren't those who predict the future but those who adapt to its twists and turns with resilience and creativity. Like Tom, you can learn to dance with uncertainty rather than fight it.

From Chapter 8: Driving Change Through Accountability

Accountability isn't punishment; it's empowerment. When everyone from the C-suite to the front line takes ownership of both problems and solutions, organizations don't just survive—they soar.

The Final Winning Move: Being Human

As we close this book, I want to share one last story. This one's about a CEO I worked with who had achieved everything on paper—market domination, record profits, industry accolades—but felt empty inside. His team performed out of fear rather than inspiration, and turnover was becoming a serious problem.

During our first session, he asked me, "What's the one thing I should change to be a better leader?"

I looked at him and said, "Start bringing cookies to your meetings."

He stared at me like I'd suggested he show up in a clown costume. "Cookies? I'm running a billion-dollar company, not a bake sale."

"Exactly," I replied. "And that's the problem. Your team knows you as a balance sheet wizard but not as a human being. Cookies are just the beginning."

He thought I was crazy, but he tried it. And no, cookies didn't magically transform his leadership overnight. But they did something important—they signaled vulnerability, care, and a willingness to step outside the CEO stereotype. It opened the door to more authentic conversations, which led to deeper understanding, which eventually transformed his leadership approach.

Six months later, his employee engagement scores had risen 40%, and he told me, "I thought leadership was about being perfect. Turns out it's about being present."

Your Next Chapter Starts Now

As you close this book and return to your leadership challenges, remember that the journey doesn't end here—it's just beginning. You now have a toolkit of principles, practices, and perspectives to guide you, but the real learning happens when you apply them in your unique context.

There will be days when you nail it—when your vision inspires, your team collaborates seamlessly, and your decisions prove brilliantly prescient. Celebrate those moments!

And there will be days when you stumble—when your communications miss the mark, your adaptability falters, or your accountability slips. Learn from those moments. They're not failures; they're feedback.

The greatest leaders I've known aren't perfect—they're practiced. They've developed the muscle memory of reflection, adjustment, and growth that turns setbacks into steppingstones.

You already have everything you need to be the leader your team deserves. Your North Star is within you. Your capacity for connection is within you. Your courage to embrace uncertainty, foster diversity, cultivate genius, and drive accountability—it's all within you, waiting to be activated.

So go lead. Not perfectly, but purposefully. Not with all the answers, but with all the right questions. Not from a position of unassailable authority, but from a place of genuine service.

And maybe bring cookies occasionally. It doesn't hurt.

Winning Takeaways

- **Leadership Is a Journey, Not a Destination**: There is no graduation day from leadership school; the best leaders remain lifelong students of their craft.
- **People Over Process, Always**: Systems, strategies, and structures matter, but they mean nothing without the hearts and minds of the people who bring them to life.
- **Your Greatest Leadership Tool Is Authenticity**: People follow real humans with real strengths and real vulnerabilities, not carefully constructed leadership personas.
- **Lead from Purpose, Not Position**: Your title gives you authority, but your purpose gives you influence—and influence is where real leadership happens.
- **Connection Creates the Conditions for Excellence**: When people feel seen, valued, and connected to something larger than themselves, extraordinary performance becomes possible.
- **The Best Leaders Create More Leaders**: Your ultimate legacy isn't what you accomplish but who you develop and how they carry your influence forward.
- **Leadership Is Love in Action**: Not the romantic kind, but the courageous kind that puts others' growth and wellbeing at the center of your leadership practice.

Winning Success Steps

- **Design Your Leadership Learning Journey**: What aspect of your leadership most needs development right now? How will you intentionally grow in that area over the next 90 days?

- **Create Your Connection Strategy**: How can you deepen authentic connections with your team members? What regular practices will ensure you're leading people, not just managing tasks?
- **Develop Your Reflection Rhythm**: When and how will you pause to assess your leadership impact? What questions will you ask yourself to ensure you're growing from experience?
- **Clarify Your Leadership Legacy**: Beyond results and achievements, what lasting impact do you want to have on the people you lead? How will they describe your leadership years after working with you?
- **Commit to Your Next Bold Move**: What one leadership principle from this book will you implement immediately? How will you measure its impact and refine your approach?

BONUS LEADERSHIP RESOURCES True influence starts with emotional connection. Use these three heart-centered leadership assessments to deepen trust, strengthen loyalty, and lead with both power and vulnerability.

Scan the QR code for your leadership-from-the-heart assessments.

Email me at
sherry@thewinningleadershipcompany.com
to book a **free** 45-minute session.

People don't follow titles. They follow truth.

Thank you for joining me on this journey. Remember, you're not just leading a team, a division, or a company. You're leading a collection of human beings with dreams, fears, talents, and potential. When you honor that reality, you transform from a manager who achieves results to a leader who leaves a legacy.

Now go be the leader they'll remember—not just for what you helped them achieve but for who you helped them become.

Sherry Winn

Acknowledgments

This book would not be what it is without the generosity of the extraordinary leaders who allowed me to step into their world and learn from their experiences. Each person I interviewed took precious time out of their demanding schedules to share not just their strategies, but their hard-earned wisdom, their challenges, and their triumphs. Their openness, vulnerability, and clarity elevated the stories within these pages from theory to truth. I am deeply grateful for their candor, their courage, and their commitment to shaping what real leadership looks like. These conversations were not just interviews—they were masterclasses in business brilliance and human connection. To each of you: thank you for being part of this journey, and for helping illuminate the path for leaders who dare to build something lasting.

Aaron Battista, Chief Retail Officer, TRP Co

Aaron McGarry, Strategic Infrastructure & Energy Partnerships, Google

Ajay Lakhwani, Chief Commercial Officer, Zapp

Ajay Pathak, COO, AmTrust International Underwriter

Alessandro Onano, Chief Marketing Officer, Moneyfarm

Alex Galho, Chief Information Officer, Vivest

Alex Quilici, CEO, YouMail

Alissa Tambone, Director of Market Research, GoDaddy

Amanda Nevins, CFO, Active Prospect

Amrit Singh, President, Field Operations, Multiplier Technologies

Anand Vidyanand, Chief Business Officer, Firework

Andrew Farrell, Senior Vice President, Symetra

Andrew Ting, Chief Legal Officer and Corporate Secretary, Panorama Education

Angelo D'Alessandro, Founder & CEO, BELLA

Anitha Bakhtani, Senior HR Director, CAE

Anna Pereira, Chairwoman, Soul Ventures

April Yearby, National Business Development Manager, Daimler Truck Financial Services USA LLC

Arun Kumar, Global Head of Data & AI, Accenture Song

Aurelien Mottier, Co-Founder & CEO, Operatix

Avy-Loren Cohen, CEO/Business Advisor, ALC Strategic Business Consulting

Bart Miller, Owner, I DO EPIC

Bill Glenn, Senior VP Marketing, Esper

Bill Tennant, Chief Revenue Officer (CRO), BlueCloud

Bill Thompson, COO, TechMD

Bill Wilshire, COO, Single Digits, Inc.

Blu Nordgren, Senior Customer Events Manager, Planet DDS

Brad Roderick, Executive Vice President, Emerald Prairie Health

Bradley Greer, Vice President, Data Solutions & Product Marketing, NetNumber Global Data Services

Brandon Sawalich, CEO & President, Starkey Hearing

Brandon Taylor, Chief Revenue Officer (CRO), Pavilion

Brent Kedzierski, Chief Learning Officer, Humanwrks

Brian Allen, Co-Founder, Optimized Outcome Solutions

Brittany Winner, EVP, J. Galt

Bryce A. James, CEO, AUDiFYZ

Cameron Jones, Chief Strategy & Commercial Officer, SilverRail

Cameron Miller, Chief Executive of Business Strategy & Innovation, Non-GMO Project

Carlos Eduardo Benitez, CEO, BMP

Carlos Vasquez, Executive Senior Partner, MassMutual Greater Washington

Casey Christopher, Business Banking Sales Leader, KeyBank

Catherine Heckler, Chief Retail/Digital Officer, Peoples Security Bank & Trust Company

Chandy Ghosh, CEO, Sinch

Chris Cooper, Fractional CISO, Rougemont Security

Chris Maset, Director, BI WORLDWIDE

Chris O'Neil/Joe Gaca, Owners, Kellogg Supply Company

Chris Zuczek, Chief Product Officer, CAIS

Christine Beeler, Program Executive Officer, U.S. Army PEO STRI

Christine Wallace, Sr. Director, Donor Relations & Engagement, OXY Occidental College

Christopher Adjei-Ampofo, Chief Information Officer, Uphold Inc.

Christopher Zuczek, Chief Product Officer, CAIS

Claude Bordeleau, CEO, VOLTA

Clinton Reilmann, CFO, Wall Colmonoy

Cory Brymer, Founder & CEO, BryComm, LLC

Cynthia Kleinbaum Milner, Chief Marketing Officer, MoneyLion

Dan Lester Sr., Vice President of Field Culture & Inclusion, Clayco

Daniel O'Keeffe, Chief Product Officer, O'Neill

Danny Olmes, CRO, Xcelerate Solutions

Daricus Releford, CEO & Founder, Storecash

Darius Janulionis, CEO & President, RETAL

Darius McDougle, CMO, GOLDLAW

Dariusz Krzeminski, EMEA HR Director, Electrical Components Int'l

Dave Bowden, Chief Information Security Officer, Frontdoor, Inc.

Dave Olsen, Founder & CEO, Nimbl

David Germann, VP/Sales & Marketing, CU LIFT Fund

David Griffith, Chairman, Modern Group Ltd

David Stiffman, Principal, Stiffman Consulting

Dean Sapp, SVP, Information Security, Privacy, Risk and Compliance (DPO), Filevine

Debbi Ann Morrissette, Director of Content-Live Events, Neuroscience Education

Deepa Bastante, Global Head of Cloud Platform, MassMutual

Dessa Glasser, Principal Consultant, FRG

Dohoon Lee, CEO, Dengyo USA

Donavan Hutchinson, Founder & CEO, D&A Services International Ltd

Douglas Eze, Founder & CEO, Largo Financial Services LLC

Dr. Kate Watson, President and Founder, The Advocacy Academy

E. Jay Hussein, VP, Global Head of Customer Office, Panorays

Edgar Escobar, CIO, ALTO

Edmund Frey, Founder and Managing Partner, Edventure Capital GmbH

Eduardo Costa, CEO, Loungerie Intimate

Edward E. Mosley, CEO, Limitless Bounds LLC

Edward Gargano, Founder & CEO, Gargano Communications

Eleni Tio, VP People Operations, Prosum

Emilyn Doria, HR Director, LG Electronics

Eric Lubow, Chief Technology Officer, MAPP

Evan Carlson, Chief Operating Officer, EasyVista

Federico Helman, CEO, imed

Fernando Araya Remagni, Co-founder & CEO, Tenpo

Francisco Diazluna, CIO, Producers National Corporation

Frank DePaola, Vice President, Chief Information Security, ENPRO

Frank Pettinato, CEO, Avantive Solutions

Gary Fan, Executive Vice President, COO, Royal Business Bank

Georgina Owens, Chief Technology Officer, William Hill International

Gerard Champi, President, Peoples Security Bank & Trust Company

Gerard Mulder, Former CEO, Tetkernel

Gerry Singleton, President & CEO, Montana's Credit Unions

Gideon Fourie, Group Chief Commercial Officer, RS2

Gillian Cummings-Beck, VP of Risk Management, Taylor Morrison

Greg Baker, Managing Partner, Alumni Ventures

Greg Leos, General Manager, Weave

Gregg Flecke, Managing Director, Kore1

Gregg Hammann, CEO, Action Advisors

Guy Warren, Former CEO, ITRS

Gustavo Ernesto Rodriguez DeLira, CEO, IT Capital

Harish Goyal, CEO & Managing Director, Essel Group

HD Jacobs, Senior Sales Executive, Q2

Henry Archibong, Head of Interoperability & Innovation, HealthMark Group

Henry Tirri, Chief Technology Officer, Nokia Technologies

Hobart Birmingham III, Managing Director, Corporate Finance Associates

Hobart McK. Birmingham, Managing Director, Corporate Finance Associates

Ian Simm, Founder/CEO, Impax Asset Management

Ismail Elshareef, Chief Product Officer, CarGurus

Issac Roybal, Chief Marketing Officer, Seclore

Jake Braly, CRO, Krisp.ai

James Gateau, Advisory Board Member, Polaron Analytics

Jason Holland, Chief Business Officer, Firework

Jason Wilcox, Chief Technology Officer, Source Advisors

Jay Nathan, COO, Churnkey.co

Jay Tkachuk, Executive Vice President, Chief Digital Officer, Golden1 Credit Union

Jeevan Varughese, CTO, Architect

Jeff Parker, Chief Executive Officer, Paymentology

Jeff Sills, Adjunct Professor, Fordham Gabelli School of Business

Jeff Wilk, Managing Director, Oyster Consulting, LLC.

Jemima Bird, CEO & Chair of Remco, Hello Finch & Pendragon PLC

Jenna Pipchuk, Chief Revenue Officer (CRO), CRO Syndicate

Jennifer O'Carroll, COO, HansaWorld

Jerzy Biernacki, Chief AI Officer, Miquido

Jesse Q. Allen, President, Reverse Mortgage Lending, Rate

Jessica Lovell, SVP, Director of Customer Relations, First National Bank Texas

Joan Ford, Managing Partner, Strategic Management Group

Joe Fijak, Global EVP/COO, Ennoconn Corporation

Joe Sanchez, Chief Revenue Officer (CRO), MotorK

Joe Tomco, President and Co-Founder, Emmersion

Joe Topinka, CEO, CIO Mentor

John Gardiner, COO & CFO, Pantheon Platform

John Harrison, CEO, Community Mediation Services

John JT Scott, VP - Enterprise Products & Services, McDonald's

John Tunison, CFO, Soluna

John-Paul Surdo, President, Bystronic Group

Johnny Russo, Chief Digital Officer (CDO), Lamour

Josh Folds, Chief Banking Officer, Fidelity Bank LA

Joshua Zable, Chief Marketing and Strategic Planning Officer, Member of Board of Directors, Minitab

Karen Brookman, President and CEO, WCD (formerly West Canadian Digital Imaging)

Karen Holliday, President, NYAK Consulting, LLC

Kate Ross, CTO, Connected Places Catapult

Kate Watson, President/Founder, The Advocacy Academy

Kaytek Przybylski, Chief Digital Officer (CDO), Lantern

Kelli Williams, CEO, The Brand Lab

Kellie Snyder, Chief Customer Officer, Onapsis

Kelly Lindsey Isikoff, Managing Director US CISO, RBC

Ken Burrough, CEO & Founder, Business Solutions

Ken Sebastian, Business Development Account Executive, Chime

Kendall Holbrook, CEO, Dev Technology Group, Inc.

Kevin Bingham, Chief Data & Analytics Officer, Chesapeake Employers'

Kevin Cutter, Arizona President, Sunwest Bank

Kevin Hinkle, CFO, Lone Mountain Land Company

Kevin Magee, Chief Technology Officer, All human

Kevin Magee, Chief Technology Officer, Intent HQ

Kim Lewis, President & CEO, United Way of Yellowstone County

Kimberly Kaminski, Chief Marketing Officer, Lakeside Software

Kristin Slanina, Former COO, ParkMyFleet

Kyle Van Pelt, Co-Founder and CEO, Milemarker

Kyle Whitehill, Chief Executive Officer, Avanti Communications Group plc

Lance Johnson, Chief Supply Chain Officer, Baxter Planning

LaSalle Vaughn, Chief Compliance & Ethics Officer, Bestow

Lauren Weiner, Chief Growth Officer, WWC Global

Lisa Hohman, CEO, Concordance Healthcare Solutions

Lisa Kinney, VP/Enterprise Analytics, Albertsons

Lori Brigg, Chief Revenue Officer, Raven.io

Lucas Sanches, CEO, Yandeh

Lyndon Docherty, Chief Executive, HiveMind Network

Maca Gomez Silva, Executive Director, Global 66

Marcelino Moreno, Chief Product Officer, Stream

Maria Johnson, CEO, M. Johnston Consulting, LLC

Marjorie Stewart-Hart, VP, Patient Engagement and Advocacy, Sage Therapeutics

Mark Hope, President, EAVX

Mark Morgan SR HR Manager Corporate Safety, NextEra Energy (retired)

Mark Powers, Chief Operating Officer, Franklin IQ

Martin Mazur, Consultant | Coach | Speaker, Mazur & Co.

Mary Boyd, CEO, Hiscox USA

Mary Byrne, COO, Immuta

Mats Nygren, VP | Sr. Manager » Enterprise Security Architecture, U.S. Bank

Matt Higgins, CEO, RSE Ventures

Matthew Hirst, Chief Executive Officer, ESG

Maverick A. Young, Founder and CETO, MAYAi Holdings

Megan Amos, Sr. Director Customer Experience, GlobalVet Link

Megan Hull, Dr. Director of Event Logistics/Operations, Big Red Media

Michael Bell, Executive Partner, Gartner

Michael Cane, Chief Manufacturing Officer, Framebridge

Michael Waite, Consultant | Strategic Advisor | COO | CFO, Waite Partners LLC

Michelle Grant, Founder, Lively and Gorgie

Miguel Oliveira, Chief Business Officer, Gamigo

Mike Kovar, Chief Financial Officer and Treasurer, Acra Lending

Mike Pallot, Global Vice President, SUSE

Mike Riggin, VP, Banking; Chief Risk Officer & CCO, Global Holdings

Mike Tannenbaum, Front Office Insider, ESPN

Mike Wallace, Chief Decarbonization Officer (CDO), Persefoni

Mita Gupta, EVP and Global Business Unit Head, WNS

Mitja Ucakar, CDO, Neos Tech

Monica Flick, Director of Events, V. Sattui Winery

Morgan Flagler, Managing Partner, Silverton Partners

Nadim Antar, Chief Revenue Officer, Striim

Neetu Jhaj, Founder & Designer, Rehna Raiya

Nicole Torraco, Former President, Xerox Financial Services

Oleg Klapovskiy, Chief Publishing Officer, Techland

Patty Contreras, Founder/CEO, The Sterling Insurance & Financial Group

Pavel Kilovatiy, CTO, Beamer

Peggy Tsai, Chief Data Officer, BigID

Phanni Pydimarri, CAO/CDO, Health Care Service Corporation

Prakash Ramachandran, Chief Financial Officer, Mode Mobile

R.S. Raghavan, CEO, Animaker Inc.

Rachel Rogers, Chief Project & Solutions Delivery Officer, Strategic Customer Products, MagMutual

Rachel Tubbs, Marketing & Events Manager, Independent Security Evaluators

Radhika Venkatraman, Senior Managing Director, Cerberus Capital Management

Rainer Waiblinger, CTO, K&P Computer Service

Ralph Dangelmaier, CEO, Strategic Advisor, Bluesnap

Ramesh Jayachandran, Executive Vice President, Million Mindz Corporation

Ramon Zapata, SVP & Chief Financial Officer, Novartis BioMedical Research

Randeep Gupta, Principal Solutions Architect, CITIZ3N

Rebecca A. Woods, CEO, Propel Health Advisors

Renaud Perrier, Chief Product Officer, Once For All

Renee Miller, Founder, The Miller Group

Rich Rogers, President & CEO, On Course Insurance

Rich Walker, CEO, Quik!

Rick Geloff, CPA

Rita Lazar-Tippe, Chief Digital Officer, Cashco Financial

Rob Cochran, President & CEO, #1 Cochran Automotive

Rob Hornbuckle, CIO, Innovative Defense Technologies (IDT)

Rob Thomas, President & CEO, WaterRock Financial Network

Robert Dorans, Director of Information Technology, Frederick Goldman, Inc.

Robert Felt, Sales Manager, Heartland Payment Systems

Robert Flores, CIO, Global Insight

Robert Kazmi, Chief Revenue Officer (CRO), Koombea

Robin Daniels, Chief Business & Product Officer, Zensai

Robin Doyle, President, Doyle Advisory

Ron Kuriscak, Field CISO, Online Business Systems

RS Raghavan, CEO & Founder, Animaer Inc.

Ruby Deol, COO & CFO, AlertEnterprise

Sabrina Bailey, CEO, Fuducient Advisors

Sally Mueller, Co-Founder, Chief Executive Officer, Womaness

Sally Stevens, Senior Business Analyst, Silicon Valley Bank

Sandra Clark, CEO, Blue Shield of California

Sanja Licina, President, QuestionPro Workforce, QuestionPro

Sanjeev Kumar, CEO, Eficens Systems

Scott Delaney, CEO & President, Unichem Laboratories Limited

Scott Kolman, former HR Executive, Fenice Community Media Group

Sonia Martinez, Chief Marketing Officer, SambaSafety

Stan Sorensen, Senior Vice President and Chief Marketing Officer, Altabank

Stephen Dawson, Vice President, Riverbed Technology

Stephen McGee, Chief Executive Officer, Scottish Friendly

Stephen Popper, SVP & Managing Director, SageView Advisory Group

Steve Hankins, CFO, Morgan Foods, Inc.

Steve MacKenzie, Chief Innovation Officer, Momentus Technologies

Steve Midgley, Group GM, Atos

Steven Rutgers, Chief Commercial Officer (CCO), Arianespace

Steven Moy, CEO, L&C New York

Stiverson Palma, Chief Executive Officer, Certsys Tecnologia da Informação

Suzanne Shaw, Senior Director, Conferences and Events, West End Tower, Vanderbilt University

Synita Gates, Program Director of Operations, University of Notre Dame

Tam Khuu, Chief Financial Officer, Wave HQ

Tarun Gupta, Project Lead, Principal Systems Architect, The Lubrizol Corporation

Thierry Jaffry, Chief Growth Officer, SOVRA

Tim Haag, CEO, State Collection Service

Tim Kuhn, CFO, Wave HQ

Tink Taylor, Founder & President, dotdigital Group PLC

Tom Spano, Sr. Director, Global Event Marketing, MNTN

Tue Sottrup, CEO, Smart Role

Tunde Cserhaime Toth, Group HR Director, MET Holding AG

Velinda Cox, SVP eCommerce, Agile Chief Product Owner (CPO), Konica Minolta Business Solutions U.S.A., Inc.

Victoria MacDonald, Chief Human Resources Officer, Wave HQ

Vidya Moore, Client Partner/GCP Practice Leader, Cloud, Data & AI, Capgemini

Vladimir Bendikow, Chief Data Officer, FBN Bank

Wanda Prewitt, CEO, SafeGuard Global

Wayne Liu, Chief Growth Officer, President of America, Perfect Corp

Werner Kruger, VP of Data & Technology Enablement, Yoco

Yatish Uchil, Head of Data and Analytics Services, BNY

Zara Nanu, Founder, WorkVue